Starting Over Single

a guide for
PREVIOUSLY MARRIED LATTER-DAY SAINTS

Starting Over
Single

a guide for
PREVIOUSLY MARRIED LATTER-DAY SAINTS

CFI
Springville, Utah

ISBN 13: 978-1-59955-128-9

Published by CFI, an imprint of Cedar Fort, Inc., 2373 W. 700 S., Springville, UT 84663
Distributed by Cedar Fort, Inc., www.cedarfort.com

LIBRARY OF CONGRESS CATALOGING-IN-PUBLICATION DATA

Read, Teena, 1939–
    Starting over single : a guide for previously married Latter-day Saints /
by Teena Read.
        p. cm.
    ISBN 978-1-59955-128-9 (alk. paper)
    1. Divorce—Religious aspects—Mormon Church. 2. Divorced
people—Religious life. 3. Divorced people—Life skills guide. I. Title.

    BX8643.D58R43 2008
    248.8'460882893—dc22

                                    2008008654

Cover design by Angela Olsen
Cover design © 2007 by Lyle Mortimer

Printed in the United States of America

10 9 8 7 6 5 4 3 2 1

Printed on acid-free paper

Dedicated with love and admiration to

John, my best friend and the love of my life,
and to Bill and Carolyn Reese,
Lowell and Debbie Fugal,
and Eric and Grace Read

All are faithful children of God who valiantly overcame
disappointment, heartbreak, and the personal devastation of starting over single and went on to fill their lives
with love and happiness.

Table of Contents

Chapter 1

Suddenly Single

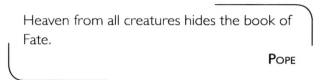

Heaven from all creatures hides the book of Fate.

POPE

It's rush hour. Headlights glare off of wet pavement. The squeal of brakes and tires skidding, and the terrible, sickening sound of metal tearing and glass breaking, interrupts the monotony of the after-work traffic.

Across town, a muffled sob intrudes upon a hushed and somber vigil. Weary, tearful eyes see that the light on the heart monitor has become the long anticipated straight line. Months of waiting and praying finally draw to a peaceful close.

Earlier in the day, in the solemnity of a courtroom, a distinguished looking man in a black robe pounded a gavel and declared soberly, "Divorce granted."

By chance or by choice, three different scenarios with a common outcome. Suddenly that individual who previously occupied some part of nearly every waking thought, influenced almost every decision, and was the giver or the recipient of countless little personal services, is gone. Where there were two, there is now only one, and we—who were married—face the task of rebuilding a life alone.

Virtually every married person will one day face the ordeal of becoming a single adult again, since not many couples depart this life together. Whether this results from an accident, an illness, or by decree, it is the same. When a temporal marriage ends, the impact is profound, even if the event was anticipated. And when that moment of separation comes, we are suddenly thrust into a world most of us have not occupied for many years. A world that is very different from the one we left behind when we said our "I do's."

Everything about being single—after having been married—seems completely different and much more complicated than the experience of a single adult anticipating marriage. The trauma of becoming a single Latter-day Saint adult also includes a set of especially painful and difficult circumstances, such as the family orientation of the Church, the stigma attached to divorce, and perhaps the difficulty of eventually finding another suitable mate from among other Church members. These prospects can be overwhelming when viewed from a position of grief.

As these things catapult into our consciousness, the emotional impact can be overwhelming. A sudden sense of total vulnerability may settle in like a shroud. And as the days drift by, we face the realization that no aspect of our life will escape the effects of losing our mate.

Emotionally, most of us are a wreck and will usually be so for some time, regardless of the event that triggered our singleness. Feelings come with such intensity and in such variety. Whether by death or divorce, the loss of a mate—who was like an extension of our very selves—can create an emotional roller coaster. We're up one minute, down the next. Or worse, we go down and stay there: it's called depression. Loneliness can be overwhelming at times and unrelenting. Holidays and birthdays can seem unbearable.

The death of a spouse can also create intense feelings of abandonment, anger, or sometimes guilt, which are perfectly normal reactions. But in our pain, we may forget that. We only know that we hurt. One widower told me that when his wife died, his heart felt like it had been ripped from his chest. Relief—in the form of heartbreak—came afterward, he said.

Some people—especially men reared in an era when boys were taught that it's not manly to cry—find it very difficult to allow themselves to show their emotions. Nevertheless, these emotions will show up sooner or later, in some form or another. And when they do, it may be hard to realize the true source if these come out as physical ailments or behavioral anomalies.

Even if one becomes single again by choice, the emotional burden of divorcing a mate is not diminished; frequently it is intensified by feelings of failure or regret. The person who was divorced can be doubly traumatized, experiencing a tremendous loss of self-esteem and confidence.

Spiritually, we may find ourselves at an all-time low once the reality of our situation begins to settle in on us. It may seem difficult even to find solace in prayer, in having had a temple marriage, or in the comfort of family members and compassionate friends. The divorced individual—whether the plaintiff or the defendant—faces a whole different set of challenges and is frequently bereft of much of the support generally offered to the widow or widower. We may find it hard to remember that the gospel is about saving individuals, in light of the emphasis placed on the family unit.

When tragedy and disappointment strike, some of us turn toward God, while others turn away. Sometimes we swing back and forth, depending on how our day is going. It's hard to understand why we've been called upon to deal with circumstances that may at times seem beyond our capacity to endure. Some of us wonder if these situations are some form of punishment for having lived imperfect lives.

When we're distraught, depressed, or angry—or experiencing any of the myriad other negative emotions that frequently beset us at times like these—it's very difficult to feel the calming, hopeful influence of the Spirit.

Socially, as single individuals, we may feel that we're something of a misfit. That person with whom we did virtually everything—our companion for Church functions, our date for dinner and a movie with friends, the one who stood next to us in the reception line, our confidant, and even our best friend—is no longer there.

And, down the road, when we begin to feel that we might be ready to socialize again, as members of the Church we are somewhat limited. If we do date, we date other Latter-day Saints. We don't go to bars (where other singles often congregate to socialize) because we don't drink alcohol or smoke, or care to frequent establishments where this takes place. We're picky about our choice of entertainment, avoiding activities like R-rated movies. And finally, we don't participate in sexual relations outside of marriage.

In a manner of speaking, the previously married Latter-day Saint is a rather strange duck in today's society.

To compound matters, we've usually been out of circulation too long to have an existing circle of single friends, and we may feel too old, too tired, or too overwhelmed with responsibilities for an ambitious effort to change that situation. (Thank goodness for the singles programs of the Church, or some of us would never do anything!) But even the social opportunities afforded singles in the Church are limited. This is still a family-oriented Church. Most previously married members feel a bit alienated, at least at first; rather like the proverbial third wheel. The married members don't quite know what to say or how to act around the newly single person. So they avoid us or, bless them, they attempt awkward conversation. The unfortunate increase in recent years of previously married members has raised awareness, and the Church has made valiant efforts to better meet the needs of single adult members. But it's sometimes hard to remember that one person alone still constitutes a family.

Financially, the newly single person may find himself or herself either substantially better off (from insurance proceeds and so forth) or significantly worse off. Seldom will finances be unaffected. Some who have had little or no involvement in family finances find themselves thrust into managing their family's money. And there can be debts that must be satisfied. The situation might demand radical changes in lifestyle. We might have to leave a well-loved home and abandon treasured belongings, or even face relocation to another city to be closer to supportive family members. A woman might have to obtain employment outside the home after years of raising children. A man's income might have to be stretched to cover the cost of maintaining two homes and payment of alimony or child support. The financial consequences of becoming single again can be disastrous.

Physically, the loss of a mate can also be devastating. As humans, most of us are social beings who require the companionship and close association of others to maintain our well being. We have a real need for physical contact. Suddenly, there is a terrible void. No hand to hold on the walk up to the chapel door on Sunday. No snuggling in the dark at the movies. No one beside us in the bed to cuddle up to until the sheets warm up.

Where physical contact of all kinds used to exist, there is only empty space and barrenness. And then there is the loss of sexual activity. Whether sex was a big part of our married life, the fact is, it's simply not there anymore. Sooner or later, this is going to become a glaring reality to be acknowledged, because our feelings don't just shut down.

There is even an intellectual impact, because with the loss of our mate, life suddenly requires that a new set of choices be made. Choices we thought we'd already made and would not have to make again. Surprise!

This transition process encourages us to cling (sometimes desperately) to the iron rod, because it is the only position that grants us an eternal perspective on everything happening in our lives. And without that eternal perspective, the trials and the challenges we face can be overwhelming, even with the knowledge that "it must needs be, that there is opposition in all things" (2 Nephi 2:11).

A key element in successfully navigating through this journey is the belief that it is possible for something good to come out of the confusion and the pain of the passage. We need to recognize in advance that the choices we make, our attitude during the trip, and how well we anticipate our needs along the way will determine, to a great extent, whether we wind up in the place we want to be.

The road we must travel as we're starting over single will probably include many byways, blind curves, and hairpin turns. There might be small bumps and some very large potholes. The enticements may be many, and sometimes the rewards seem few. It is a road that will undoubtedly feel very lonely at times, and sometimes the burden of decision-making may be overwhelming. But it is a journey that can lead to a place of true happiness, peace, and contentment.

There is no option about whether to make the transition. Like it or not, it must be done. The only option really open to us is in determining the eventual outcome. And therein lies the opportunity!

There is a promise in the scriptures that "all things work together for good to them that love God" (Romans 8:28). All things! That can include the painful experience of finding ourselves single again after the loss of a mate. By applying that promise, we know it is possible to have a successful transition in building a new and fulfilling life. And we can find happiness as a single, previously married member of the Church.

Chapter 2
Attitude Is Everything

For as he thinketh in his heart, so is he.

PROVERBS 23:7

Is the glass half full or half empty?

Whether the question is about how we see that well-known glass of water or about viewing our situation in life, it's usually all a matter of perspective.

It's a simple fact that we cannot always control life's challenges, but we can choose our responses. And these choices include not only what we do, but also what and how we think—in other words, our attitude.

Even though it may be hard, we must believe in the future and what it holds for us. Sometimes it may be the only way we can overcome the grief and the stress of the present.

Try to think of your future happiness in terms of what we learned as children. Remember how amazed you were on that rainy day when your mother or father told you that the sun was always shining somewhere, even while dreary skies or storms blocked your view of it at the moment? Even though it may be difficult, we need to remember that happiness is always out there, perhaps just out of view. The dark clouds occupying our skies right now only temporarily block it from our view. We need to believe in that future happiness.

This can seem difficult—even impossible—to grasp and accept when our heart is full of pain and we're mired in the depths of depression that so often accompany the loss of a loved one. Depression does not discriminate depending on the circumstances surrounding our loss. It can come to the widow and the widower, to the divorcing person and the person divorced. The deeper the depression, the harder it is to see the end of it, or to even image that life could possibly hold happiness for us ever again.

But while our future happiness might not be clearly visible now, it *will* inevitably come again, so we have to be ready for it when it arrives! A positive attitude will lighten the burdens of the day and offer the greatest assurances of a positive outcome to all we're experiencing right now.

Whether our loved one has died or we have gone through a divorce, we've suffered a terrible loss. In either event, there is a grieving process; but it won't last forever. Time will take care of some of it, but in the meantime, there are many things we can do to help ourselves to move through those phases of grief. Shoring up our faith will be imperative in helping us improve our attitude.

From our present perspective, so many of the things that might help us may seem pointless and without meaning. Or they might seem to require more effort and energy than we can muster.

So much of the advice that we receive seems so trite. Well-meaning friends offer us platitudes and panaceas, and (we're convinced) they don't really have a clue about what we're going through. *You* might feel exactly this way about what you read next, but I promise you that it's true. I know, because it worked for me and it has worked for countless others who have been where you might be right now. Place your whole trust in the Lord, believing with all your heart that he will direct your paths and prosper your righteous endeavors (see Proverbs 3:5–6; Helaman 12:1).

One of the things we can do to jump-start a more positive attitude is to begin looking for the blessings that will eventually come of this experience, because those blessings *will* be there. Heavenly Father knows our capacity and has assured us that he will never give us more than we can bear. (Some of us have had occasions to remind him of that promise!) His plan for our growth often proceeds along a time frame that's different from our own. Relief from tribulation can be just days, hours, or even moments away. At times like these our job is simply to hang on until it comes, believing with all our hearts that it will come, because when we keep his commandments, he is bound to keep his promises (see D&C 82:10).

When you make the choice to actively seek out happiness—the choice not to remain depressed—it is, in reality, a decision to take charge of your life again, to become proactive in your own behalf. The very act of making this decision is liberating and empowering. And if the assistance of professional counseling or temporary medication is required to help you get through this, so be it. Just don't allow yourself to become a victim of your own emotions.

Unfortunately, some of us have become so conditioned to pain and disappointment that we've forgotten how to be happy! Or we've learned to get our comfort and support from others by retaining our unhappiness. We cling to it like an old friend, because to let go is to give up the familiar and venture out into unknown territory. Will we lose the attention of friends who now offer sympathy and encouragement? Will we be abandoned, if we're not needy? Can we even take that chance?

It's a trap that's easy to fall into while we're wading through a crisis. But be brave! Just for today, take heart in any sunny moment, no matter how small. If that's too much to ask of yourself right now, try it for an hour. Find a little joy in a spring blossom, a stranger's smile, or a sweet memory.

Even on the dreariest day, a little happiness can be found if you are willing to accept it. Grab every moment of pleasure and hang on! Soon these little snatches of happiness will get longer and longer until they become the norm rather than the exception.

The point is, we mustn't postpone our happiness! We mustn't promise ourselves, "I'll be happy when . . ." We can be happy *now*. We don't have to be giddily happy all the time; just try to let some sunshine into your soul today. We can let go of a little bit of our heartache just long enough to really *feel* a smile or a chuckle. And if we can't muster the genuine thing, we can always pretend!

I read once about a behavior modification technique called "act as if." The premise is that if you *act* happy, soon you will *be* happy. Some writer probably thought he'd discovered something new and wonderful when he set forth this principle, but really it's just another way to state that "as [a man] thinketh in his heart, so is he" (Proverbs 23:7).

So, smile at yourself in a mirror. Then grin at the person smiling back at you! At first, you might feel silly (I did). But if you'll do this for just a few minutes, you'll be amazed at the physical change you'll feel in your body. It's like a lightening of the spirit, and it doesn't take long at all.

Make yourself laugh! Try renting a stack of hilarious movies and then watch them—one after another. Just don't be like my friend Anna, who complained that she'd rented six comedies and it didn't help her depression one bit. I asked her how many of them she'd watched. She said, "Well, none, actually."

We have to follow through on our efforts if we want them to work. Read a funny novel, a joke book, or even the Sunday comics. Spend time with an old friend and talk about some of the silly times you experienced together. Do whatever makes you laugh!

There is a physiological basis for the belief that smiling makes us feel better. Researchers explain that using the smile muscles changes the direction of the blood flow through our cheeks, causing a cooling of the blood's temperature. This, in turn, inhibits the release of serotonin, a chemical that is believed to be inversely related to depression. Smiling also promotes the release of endorphins into the bloodstream. These are well known for making us feel good, the ones responsible for that euphoric state track athletes call "runners' high."

We can use this technique to fool our depressed selves into thinking that we're not depressed anymore. And wouldn't it feel good to feel good again?

Another sure way to feel better almost immediately is to look around for someone whose spirits we can lift up. Someone who is still in that awful place where we were last week, or yesterday, or earlier today. We can give our hands to God and let him direct us. We can help him answer a prayer for help from another of his children. It's been said that here on earth, God has no other hands but ours. Remember when someone came to you and it was an answer to your prayers?

By deciding to feel better, we grant ourselves permission to be happy again. Some of us need that consent. Sometimes we have goofy ideas about how someone in our situation is supposed to behave, and we act accordingly. How long *should* we mourn? How long is our grief *supposed* to last? How long before it's *okay* to be happy again?

Our mental outlook is also going to affect our physical health. And vice versa! Recognize that you're probably more susceptible to illnesses while you're working through your current situation, so get plenty of rest, eat well, and get some exercise to reduce your stress. Treat yourself with kindness but not with pity.

Accept the fact that your emotions will probably be careening around for a while, and that this is normal. It's fine to cry now and then. In fact, it's healthy and necessary to the recovery process. My counselor told me that some of the chemicals in the brain that cause depression can only leave the body through the tear ducts. That's why we feel so much better after a good cry. I don't know if it's true or not, but it sounds good!

Talking about the pain, disappointment, anger, or fear we feel in association with our current situation is necessary to the healing process, and it's okay. It's normal. But we need to remember to talk, not to wallow. My friend Patty told me after a three-year bout of depression that she didn't start to feel better until she got off what she called her "pity party." Someone who loved her sat her down and "let her have it with both barrels," she said. At the time, it was very difficult to hear, but she was grateful for such good advice. It literally changed her life.

Eric didn't have anyone to talk to about his feelings after his wife died. A sister in his ward was very sympathetic but had never experienced a single death in her family. People would ask him how he was feeling, but beyond that, he said, there wasn't much consolation. He said he found an answer that helped him, and satisfied those tentative inquiries, in a line from a Clint Eastwood movie, *The Eiger Sanction*: "We shall continue with style." Since he couldn't change what had happened, he knew he simply had to make the best of it—so he just went from day to day, and continued with style and dignity.

Some singles seem to harp endlessly on their sad tales, eventually making married people, and even other single friends, uncomfortable or bored. It might be best to try to find one or two good friends who understand your situation and can handle it, and then try to limit yourself to confiding in them.

This is also where professional counseling can be very beneficial, especially in helping you get some perspective on what has happened to you. There are a variety of counseling options available: private, if you have good insurance; community mental health programs that frequently charge on a sliding scale or are free; grief support groups; divorce support groups; groups for single parents; even support groups for persons who have lost loved ones through violent crimes. LDS Family Services counselors understand the range of special circumstances surrounding a Latter-day Saint's loss of a mate. See your bishop if you think this might be your best hope.

Barbara, a thirty-year-old widow with two children, enlisted professional help during her transition. She found it useful between appointments to write down the issues she was having difficulty coping with or working through. Then she'd go as far as she could trying to work things out on her own. When she reached a plateau, she saw her counselor again with a list of unresolved items to cover. After a brief explanation of her current situation, Barbara could get right down to business with the issues she couldn't handle alone. It saved time, money, and emotional energy because she didn't have to rehash everything before she started getting some relief.

In developing a more positive attitude about your own situation, it will probably be helpful to determine a realistic view of what you can expect from your new circumstances. Accept that things are going to be different, but remember that different doesn't necessarily mean bad. If all your expectations are realistic, you will minimize your disappointments and eliminate lots of problems and pitfalls.

There is no way around it: things will be different, but life can be full of joy and fulfillment. As plans for the future develop, you can adjust your expectations to fit your present circumstances as part of the overall plan for yourself. I promise that you will discover some very positive aspects to your new life as a single person.

Right now, your job is to shore up your faith and be believing. The Lord's promise to the Prophet Joseph also extends to each of us: "Know thou, my son, that all these things shall give thee experience, and shall be for thy good" (D&C 122:7).

A good place to start acquiring a more positive outlook could be with your physical appearance. Stand tall. Remember to smile at yourself in the mirror, every chance you get. Wear something bright and put some spring into your step. Remember to act as if you're happy. Decide to help someone else feel better by finding someone to serve. Make a welcoming phone call to that new person in the ward; write a note of appreciation for a well-taught Sunday School lesson; go weed the flower beds for the lady up the street who's recovering from hip surgery.

Make the decision to look for happiness now—not after this or that happens, not next week or next year. Right now! Become proactive in your own healing. And remember that when we're busy and involved in a good cause, there is little time for self-pity, because if we spread sunshine, some of the glow has to rub off on us.

Chapter 3

Redefining Yourself as an Individual

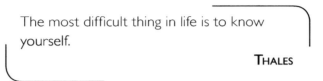

The most difficult thing in life is to know yourself.

THALES

On a brilliant October afternoon in 1983, Jennifer, a forty-three-year-old with five grown children, stepped through the doors of a courthouse into the crisp fall air. She said she could hear the sounds of the traffic and the chatter of birds gossiping in ancient oak trees that surrounded the old county building. Blinded momentarily by the sudden brightness of the autumn sun, she paused at the top of the steps beside her attorney.

"Well, Jennifer," he asked, "how do you feel?"

His question caught her off guard, she said, and she searched her mind for a response, but only one word came forth. "Smaller," she responded.

Jennifer explained to me that, somehow, she felt as if she were physically smaller than when she had entered the courthouse an hour earlier. After twenty-four years of marriage, with the striking of a gavel just minutes before, suddenly she was starting over single.

Like many women who marry young, Jennifer had progressed from being her parents' daughter to being her husband's wife and then, within the first eight years of marriage, she became a mother of five. She'd always been someone else's person. She had never really experienced life as an individual and had no idea of what that should or would feel like. There had always been someone to ask or tell if she were going somewhere, or to call if she were running late. Someone whose likes and dislikes always needed to be considered. Someone who could influence or override her decisions, limit her activities, and influence her choices.

Someone whose wants or needs often seemed more important than her own. And now, suddenly, she was on her own.

· · · · · · · · · · · · · · · ·

As the weeks and months slipped by after the death of her husband in a traffic accident, Megan found herself faced with endless choices, some of them quite mundane. These were choices that she'd never consciously had to make before, because she had almost always lovingly adapted to the preferences or needs of her husband or children. Suddenly she realized that she had choices! She could eat what and when she wanted, come and go as she pleased, get up early or go to bed late, spend an entire day reading, or stay up and sew until the wee hours.

Like Jennifer and Megan, I also discovered after my divorce that I had a whole new set of choices. It was rather strange how my awareness of this came about. During lunch with a coworker, I ordered a small chef's salad with Roquefort dressing. And all at once, I had one of those light-bulb moments, realizing that I'd been eating Roquefort dressing for over twenty years, and I don't really like Roquefort dressing!

Beginning with that revelation, I eventually recognized what I perceived to be an incredible opportunity to reinvent myself. No, wait! Not an opportunity, but an absolute necessity. I realized that I had not yet truly accepted or defined myself as an individual. In so many ways, I was continuing to live my life in still-married mode.

Each evening since the divorce, I'd gone straight home from work. I never even thought of doing anything else. I declined each time my coworkers invited me to go for a bite to eat after work or to see a movie. I'd rush home, fix dinner, and sit down to an evening in front of the TV—because it was what I'd been used to doing.

It never occurred to me that I could take up again some of the things I used to enjoy before I was married—simple things, like reading good books, attending concerts and community theater presentations, or inviting friends over to play board games, things I dearly loved to do but had abandoned years before.

Over the course of a marriage, our individual identities can become so immersed in the personality of our mate and the requirements of other family members that, as newly single persons, some of us may need to rediscover ourselves. This may be especially true for those whose

mate was the more dominant personality, and those who usually acqui-
esced when a decision was to be made or gave in just to keep the peace.

Behaviors such as these can eventually—and unwittingly—result
in the diminishing of one's own personality. We can lose our tastes,
preferences, traits, and subtle characteristics that set us apart as unique
beings. Not recognizing that we're experiencing an identity crisis can
also influence future behaviors and relationships.

When Jennifer ventured out and began to date, she seemed to grav-
itate toward men whose personality and physical builds were strongly
similar to those of her ex-husband. On some subconscious level, it
seemed more comfortable. She knew instinctively how to get along with
them, please them, and make them feel good about themselves. The
relationships didn't require any work on her part.

Once Jennifer realized what was happening, she said it was a comfort zone she wanted to get out of in a hurry! She understood that she
was headed for a potential disaster if she ever did begin to get serious
with someone.

Jennifer explained that she suddenly understood, on a very deep and
painful level, the phenomenon of certain divorced people who involve
themselves, time after time, in the same types of doomed relationships.
It's not something done intentionally; it just happens if we're not alert.

On the other hand, a ninety-year-old widowed friend had two wonderful marriages to men who could be considered "peas in a pod." They
both possessed tenderly considerate natures, integrity, and strong testimonies. So looking for the same type of man paid off for her. Each of us
knows what will work best for us.

Change is almost always difficult. Especially where relationships
are concerned. We become accustomed to someone, and over time we
learn to negotiate the relationship to maximize our happiness—or
sometimes to minimize our unhappiness. Even without being aware of
it, we might have developed a set of behaviors that allowed us to obtain
whatever it was we wanted from a previous relationship, or sometimes
just to get by. Some of us are still working through leftover anger and
pain. Others have such a reservoir of remembered positive experiences
and accomplishments that it can seem that no one, or nothing, in the
future could ever favorably compare.

That baggage—whether bad or beautiful—can come forward with us into new relationships. If we're not aware of this, and if we're not careful, we can inadvertently undermine our own chances for happiness and success in a new life. Most of us have at least some mental house cleaning to do; others of us need to do major remodeling!

For myself, the more thought I gave to my situation, the more confused I became. I realized that I was experiencing a real identity crisis, because if I were still eating Roquefort dressing, were there other areas of my life wherein I was still acting and responding from my former role? I took a hard look at myself and realized that I needed to characterize not only who and what I was at that moment, but also who and what I wanted to be for the rest of my life.

A solution to these questions evolved as I set about to write down all the things I was discovering about myself. My writing project began with "I don't like Roquefort dressing!" and went on from there until I eventually listed every trait and characteristic I could think of, the combination of which set me apart from everyone else on the planet. Eventually it became several pages long, and I called it " 'Me' by Me." (Original, don't you think?) Seeing these things in writing made me realize how little I'd honored myself throughout my adult life.

Short- and long-range goals soon began making their way into my list. I was a little tentative at first, but I was determined. First, I promised myself that I'd plan my activities each Sunday to avoid that overwhelming sense of loneliness that made me dread the weekends.

Next, I committed myself to becoming more fit, and I made a plan to begin walking for exercise. I'd already succeeded in losing almost fifty pounds over the prior twelve months, and now I wanted to feel physically strong too.

I went out on a limb with a decision to attend Campus Education Week at BYU the following summer. At the time, I had no idea where the money for this would come from, but I made the plan anyway. This goal made me think twice whenever I spent any portion of the small amount of discretionary funds available to me at that time.

Eventually I got the courage to begin looking at my past. The more time distanced me from my former life, the more clearly I seemed to see everything that had happened over the last twenty-six years. I began to realize the ways in which I'd contributed to my own unhappiness. I was understanding the true dynamics of the relationships in my family.

My own foibles became painfully clear as I began to see that I had actually unwittingly encouraged, or even consciously allowed, many of the situations that led to the breakdown of my marriage. And it was through this process that I came to accept personal responsibility for the ways that I had contributed to the problems that had plagued my marriage.

Further, I realized that it was my own willingness to relinquish my personal preferences, and my refusal to let my feelings and needs be known, that had resulted in the virtual disappearance of "me."

I began to understand that if I wanted to change the outcome of the game (my future), first I had to change my game plan.

At first, thoughts along these lines came to mind only when I made a conscious decision to think specifically about them. Soon, however, ideas began to flow, unbidden, and to capture them I dedicated a section in my journal to this effort.

Each day my knowledge about my life, my future, and myself expanded. It was uncomfortable at first, but the more I thought about these things, and the more I wrote, the easier the process became.

It wasn't a quick or easy exercise, and often it was painful. Old memories were hard to face, and I didn't always like what I discovered about myself. But I was determined to accept personal responsibility—not only for my future happiness but also for what the television attorneys call "contributory negligence." I had unwittingly contributed to the failure of my marriage.

This was a very cleansing and restorative experience for me, and I'll tell you more later about where this effort eventually led me.

When my self-definition was completed, I made two copies. I carried a copy with me and had another at my bedside. I read it first thing each morning, several times during the day, and again before my prayers each night. Everything in my life felt so tenuous at that time, and this exercise not only helped to reinforce my new single identity, but it reminded me that I was doing lots of things right, helped me work on my shortcomings, and kept my goals before me.

Little by little, day by day, my self-esteem began to return and my happiness and inner peace grew. Defining myself was one of the most beneficial things I did during my transition.

I've included my self-definition statement at the back of the book. Perhaps by reading it, you will recognize your need to do one of these for yourself and get some ideas about how you might start. But I warn you, it's very personal. When I wrote it, it was not with the intention that anyone else would ever see it.

Roquefort dressing brought about my epiphany—what will it be for you? Do you really know who you are right now? What you really like and don't like? What you want from your life? Are you stuck in another time? Are you still thinking and behaving as an extension of someone else?

If you decide that you need to redefine yourself, you might start with a small notepad you can carry around with you. Just write down whatever thoughts pop into your mind. Try to identify the characteristics and goals you want for yourself now, and those you want included in your future. And don't forget to include those things you do *not* want in your life.

Susan, whose ex-husband could never turn down an invitation to hear an off-color joke and then insisted on repeating these to her, made the decision to stop every person who asked if she wanted to hear a "good joke." She decided that if it was a dirty joke, she didn't want to hear it. Jeff, whose late wife had a terrible sweet tooth, threw out all the high-calorie snack foods and dessert mixes that had always been an indispensable part of their shopping list. One of the best things about defining yourself is that you can choose exactly who you want to be— and then you can become that person!

It's up to you. You can paint yourself into the picture of your choice. The goals you set for yourself now will determine who you will be next month, next year, or ten years from now. Why should you leave your future to chance? What do you really want from life?

Remember that wonderful behavior modification technique called "act as if . . ."? It takes a little practice, but it works like this: Once you've identified a characteristic or quality you'd like to incorporate into your own persona, you need only act as if you already possess that trait and, voila! It can be yours!

Recall how the Savior told his disciples that in order to be like him they would have to do the things they saw him do. It's the same for us. Before long, it will become second nature.

Look for people who embody the qualities and behaviors you desire, and then emulate those traits to make them your own.

You can even change role models according to your need. Do you want to be a parent who listens instead of one who constantly yells? Imitate your parenting models when you're dealing with your children, and behave as you think they should in your situation.

Become like your business model when you go in to ask for that raise, return that faulty appliance, or ask to speak to a supervisor when the customer service person is giving you the runaround. Whatever the situation, just assume the attributes of each of your role models and then act from your new self. Don't just keep reacting in the same way, from your old set of behaviors. You're the only one who will know that you're acting. And soon—sooner really than you might imagine—you won't be acting anymore. Those qualities you desire will be part of you. Comfortable, natural, and permanent.

Have you lived on the fringes of the Church, for example, and longed for the peace the Spirit brings? Use this time of your life to include a return to the comfort and safety of the gospel. Attend your meetings, do your home or visiting teaching, accept a calling or do a better job with the one you have. *Act* like a faithful Church member, and you will become one!

Do you want to be known as a compassionate person? A happy person? A patient person? Someone who sees good in everyone and everything? Who do you want to be?

Each time you succeed at a new endeavor, your confidence will grow. Each time you stumble, and then recover, you will become stronger. Rarely does a person have the opportunity to look so deeply within, to develop a better self, to create new habits, and to replace old attitudes or unacceptable, self-defeating behaviors. This will be a humbling experience but one you will come to treasure as you rediscover and redefine yourself and begin to truly bloom.

Because of the pivotal nature of the transition period, we are free to change virtually anything about ourselves. If that involves some serious talks with priesthood authorities, let it be done with expedience. Determine to face whatever needs to be faced. Don't hang on to the pain of the past after true repentance has taken place. Just look to the joy the future surely holds.

You can regard this as one of the worst times of your life, or you can regard this time of transition time as a gift, perhaps to help compensate for your loss, however that loss came about. It's really up to you.

This can be one of the real blessings that could come out of an otherwise devastating experience. Choose to take control, affirm your eternal nature as you redefine yourself as a single person and refuse to be battered about by the sheer circumstances of your life right now.

You can do this! Don't delay another day. Begin right now!

Will this be easy? No. I wish with all my heart that I could tell you it is—but it's not.

Will it be worth it? Absolutely!

Chapter 4

Some Spiritual Aspects of Being Single Again

All things . . . shall work together for your good.

D&C 98:3

In times of adversity—and this transition period certainly qualifies!—we sometimes feel utterly alone, isolated in and by our pain. It isn't always easy to keep the Lord's assurance of eternal happiness and future blessings for righteous living in the forefront of our minds when we are suffering so acutely. Sometimes we feel abandoned by the Spirit, bereft of any sense of real communion with our Heavenly Father. We vaguely remember his promise not to give us more than we can bear, but we wonder if he might have overestimated our capacity!

At times like this, it's so easy to withdraw into our suffering, to nurse our wounded hearts in a kind of solitary confinement where no comfort can penetrate. There seem to be so many broken dreams, so much disappointment and disillusionment! We've made so much effort, yet so many prayers seem unanswered! We may even question why these circumstances have devolved upon us when we've tried so hard to do what's right. Or we isolate ourselves and suffer in the prison of regret for the mistakes we've made, feeling that the Father will no longer respond to our prayers.

At this juncture, we have only two options: we can pull away, angrily shutting out the Lord for allowing our painful circumstances, or we can draw closer to him and find the solace and comfort that faith provides us.

Heavenly Father has promised that he will always be there for us, that he will never abandon us. So, if we feel a lack of his presence—for whatever reason—we can be assured that it is we who have withdrawn from him.

Adversity can humble, teach, and strengthen one who chooses to make it his servant rather than his master. The scriptures tell us that to God, all things are spiritual. Even adversity. The Prophet Joseph Smith recorded the words used by Heavenly Father to describe the consequences of adversity, as Joseph languished in the squalor of Liberty Jail. The Lord pledged to Joseph, "All these things shall give thee experience, and shall be for thy good" (D&C 122:7).

I believe that assurance applies to each of us today as much as it did to the Prophet Joseph. Everything that happens in our lives can be turned to an advantage, if we seek the spirit to help us ferret out the good. Sooner or later, those blessings will be made manifest if we believe and remain patient and watchful.

While handling a particularly sensitive Relief Society assignment, Linda, a widowed mother of three, said she was privileged on one particular occasion to realize that an experience she'd had some years earlier was given for the express purpose of preparing her to address the situation she was then dealing with. Linda said she'd had this feeling on other occasions, and I've talked to others who have shared this experience.

Linda believes that not only are we given experiences for our own benefit, but also for the benefit of others who might one day cross our paths. She has always treasured the saying "God has no other hands on earth but ours." The longer she lives, she said, the more she realizes that answers to prayers usually come through the people around us.

You will almost certainly have the opportunity to use the wisdom you gain from your own transition experiences to benefit someone in your future. Watch for and take advantage of those occasions to bless another person who is walking where you have already trod.

Being single can also provide additional opportunities to devote greater efforts to our spiritual development by virtue of the increased amount of time we have to ourselves. Once again, we have a choice. We can bemoan our solitude, or we can choose to take advantage of these quiet times to draw closer to the Lord and to help ourselves grow in the gospel.

Linda also shared with me that she recalls times when hours slipped away like minutes as she poured out her heart to Heavenly Father and sought inspiration and direction. She said that she had never before prayed with so much purpose and intensity; neither had she listened so hard for answers. Perhaps because she had never needed his guidance as desperately as she did then. As a single person, Linda learned the meaning of real communion with God.

Early in my own transition, I set a goal to read my scriptures daily, which earlier I hadn't consistently found time to do. For the first time, I found myself really studying, and the benefits were almost immediate. I found calmness, serenity, and a true inner peace that had earlier eluded me. My days went better. I made decisions with more confidence, and I lost my sense of being so alone.

Bradley, a widowed father of seven, decided he could economize on transportation by taking the city bus back and forth to work. The good news was that he saved money. The bad news was that a man who took the same bus, and who always seemed to sit near him, constantly used language Brad found very offensive. In an effort to block it out, he took a copy of the *Ensign* magazine with him one day to read on the bus.

Over the next several months, during his ninety-minute round-trip ride, Brad read through about three years' worth of *Ensign* magazines that had been gathering dust. He said he quickly gained a testimony that these contain the word of the Lord sent to us today. Whatever he needed each day, Brad seemed to find it either in the scriptures or in the *Ensign*. What a blessing! More examples that the Lord can turn *all things* to our good—even an annoying bus passenger.

If we set our minds to it, we can often find a way to turn stumbling blocks into stepping stones.

Keeping a journal is also helpful. I found that the best barometer of how I was doing seemed to be my journal. During the months of separation prior to the divorce, I began to keep a journal again, perhaps out of sheer desperation for someone to talk to—someone who wouldn't give me platitudes and a bunch of unwanted advice.

In the beginning, I poured out my pain and frustration, my fears and uncertainties, my feelings of inadequacy and failure, and especially my self-doubt every night. The journal gave me absolute confidentiality, and I could say anything I wanted. It was therapeutic, and as the months went by, I began to feel purged of some of the negative feelings that seemed to be smothering my heart.

Looking back at those pages now, I can see clearly just when I began to emerge from under that pall of despair, because I began to mention all the little things for which I was thankful each day, recognizing the ways in which my prayers were answered and, eventually, my concerns for the people around me. I had finally started to come out of myself. It was a wonderful healing experience.

A recurring theme in my daily entries became expressions of my testimony. It wasn't intentional, but it came through as simple declarations of faith and the profound gratitude that filled my heart.

As my spirit grew, so did my awareness that my life was not over because I was divorced, and that my efforts still needed to be directed toward preparing for the rest of my life—here on earth and in the eternities. The word of the prophets and the General Authorities increased my confidence in the promise that no blessing will be denied to a single member of the Church who lives worthily for that blessing.

I accepted the fact that my life was changed. It was time to move on, with hope for my future. Whatever that turned out to be, I wanted to be prepared.

Over the months, however, some uncomfortable feelings nagged at me, but I couldn't quite identify the source. Just a little something that sat there at the back of my mind. Eventually I prayed about it because I felt it was inhibiting my progress in some way.

One night, while reading the Bible, I came across the answer in the book of Matthew (6:14–15; 18:21–35). Despite my seemingly good adjustment to my divorce, I still harbored a lot of anger and resentment about things that happened in my marriage. And I knew, on an intellectual level, that I needed to let go of those feelings, and forgive my ex-husband for his part in the failure of our marriage.

This was not a revelation I took to immediately, but I accepted it in principle and began to work at it. Even though I had no idea of just how I would go about actually getting rid of all my bad feelings, I knew that if I wanted assurance of forgiveness by the Father for my own faults, I had to find a way. A few days later, I saw a bumper sticker that read, "Let Go and Let God."

In my heart that expression rang true, and I knew that I must somehow stop requiring my ex-husband to recognize his part in the breakup and be sorry before I would be willing to let go of my anger and feelings of resentment toward him. I realized that we cannot grant our forgiveness of another child of God contingent upon their repentance. That's the Lord's prerogative, not ours. Each of us is merely commanded to forgive.

Knowing this—and being able to actually do it—were two different things, and I really struggled for a time with this. Then I heard someone say that real forgiveness is giving up your desire to hurt someone who has first hurt you. Not physically, of course, but of wanting them to suffer as you have suffered. I liked hearing it put that way, and eventually I did find a way to let go of those feelings. More about that later.

The rightness of that effort to forgive was reinforced when, several weeks later, I attended the temple for the first time as a divorcée and was again reminded that we are endowed as individuals—not as couples. Our salvation, our ultimate place in the eternities, will be determined by how we perform in this life as individuals. We are accountable only for our own actions and for our own repentance. Some of us fear attending the temple for the first time as a single member, expecting that it will be an overwhelmingly emotional experience. We might put it off, thinking we can't face being there alone.

I went back the first time in the company of a dear friend who understood my circumstances, and once I was actually in the temple, I realized that I hadn't needed to worry about it. That sweet, peaceful feeling was impossible to resist. Oh, there were bittersweet memories, mixed with deep regrets, but it was wonderful to be in the house of the Lord once again.

If you've been putting off going to the temple as a single adult, please don't wait. Make an opportunity to go as soon as you can. If there is something in your life preventing you from enjoying this blessing, take some positive action soon to get yourself on the path to the temple again or for the first time. There truly is no place on earth where God is so close and the Spirit so accessible.

If you were married or sealed in the temple and are now divorced, somewhere down the line you may someday have occasion to seek a cancellation of the sealing. (I used to erroneously refer to this as getting a "temple divorce.") Of course, this is an action to be considered prayerfully and with guidance from priesthood leaders. But if you determine that this is something you need to do, your bishop's office will be the place to begin. The bishop will counsel you and provide paperwork to start the process, which then moves on to the stake president.

I was terribly intimidated by this prospect, expecting to deal with endless forms. I thought I'd be required to provide long, arduous explanations and documentation. I was surprised, but certainly not disappointed, to find the forms were few and very simple. I guess the Lord knows we've been through a wringer already, so in his loving manner he has (to use today's vernacular) made this process quite user friendly.

Friendly—now that's not an adjective I commonly associate with Heavenly Father or Jesus Christ, but they are indeed our friends. Always ready to listen, to offer peace and encouragement. Always willing to give us direction when we're feeling lost and bewildered. They are constantly there for us, offering a divine love that is never withdrawn. All it takes on our part is faith and a willingness to believe.

Believe that you will again know joy.

Believe that you can come out of this a better person.

Believe that your Heavenly Father loves you.

Believe his promise that he will bear you up and will never leave you to deal with your problems alone.

Chapter 5
Healing the Anguish

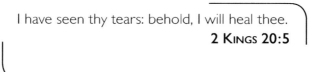

I have seen thy tears: behold, I will heal thee.
2 KINGS 20:5

The ending of any close relationship wounds us deeply, especially when it was the one between marriage partners. That worn old expression "my other half" survives each generation because it's so close to the truth. The unique nature of marriage requires the virtual merging of two souls into one being. When one partner suddenly disappears, whether by death or divorce, a tremendous void exists in the life of the survivor, who is abruptly thrust into a state of grieving.

Research has shown that everyone passes through the various stages of grief at his or her own pace. It's different for each of us. And there is almost no difference between death and divorce when considering that a real loss has occurred. Many people fail to recognize this fact. Just like the widow or widower, a divorced person will pass through a period of mourning for the death of the marriage relationship. And both will have to work through the grief process before real healing can occur.

Unless the quest for true healing is actively pursued and becomes a priority, the pain of the loss, or wounds from the old relationship, can simply be glossed over, only to intensify and flare again later.

Some of us put on a happy face to mask our pain and distress, not wishing to burden family and friends by revealing our true feelings. Or we may go to the other extreme, wallowing almost endlessly in our sorrow, inhibiting our own ability to move from one stage of grief to another, to finally emerge as a healed soul. Most of us are somewhere in between.

Close friends, within and without the Church, can be sources of strength and comfort.

Talking about your situation, your feelings, your fears, and your hopes will be necessary to your healing. Choose carefully those in whom you confide. You'll need people who will keep your confidences and give you honest feedback.

There has to be someone there to listen, but not necessarily to offer advice. These kind people can also serve as a sounding board for you, someone to bounce thoughts and ideas off while you're sorting things out. Talking aloud, rather than just mulling things over in your mind, can often help you get a better perspective.

When we fail to acknowledge all the pain that's there, and take action to work through it, it's as though we're placing a Band-Aid on our emotions instead of striving for complete recovery. This is an unfortunate compromise and a concession that can impede the healing process and postpone our successful transition into a new and rewarding life.

Whatever barriers we face—loneliness, disappointment, remorse, bitterness, anger—in moving past the pain and into a life of happiness and satisfaction once again, we need to vow to ourselves that we will use no Band-Aids!

Depression is common, but we don't always realize the true reasons behind the condition. Sometimes it's difficult to recognize when we're using avoidance tactics on ourselves. For example, it was months after Megan's husband passed away before she realized that she was angry with him for leaving her to face the rest of her life alone, with all their wonderful plans unfulfilled.

She was determined to come through this loss well, but she stranded herself in the grief process because she wanted to be strong for the sake of her family.

Her only obvious problem, as far as she could see, was a recurring cycle of depression that she just couldn't shake. Then one day she heard a therapist on talk radio say that depression is often anger turned inward. At first, she thought that couldn't possibly apply to her, since she wasn't feeling angry.

As time passed, however, Megan realized that she *was* angry. Indeed, she was very angry! And the reason for the cycle of depression was that, as her counselor put it, she kept moving her anger around from one pocket to another, instead of dealing with it once and for all.

In other words, whenever those uncomfortable feelings would start to surface, she'd find some way to temporarily get rid of them (she'd move them to another pocket where they felt less uncomfortable). Days or weeks would go by and the negative feelings would start to return, and she'd repeat the pocket-switching maneuver. It wasn't until Megan finally confronted her true feelings about the death of her husband that she was able to find resolution and peace.

John Greenleaf Whittier penned this truism: "For of all sad words of tongue or pen, the saddest are these: It might have been."

Jonathan, a fifty-nine-year-old widower who lost his wife after an extended illness, couldn't seem to shake the depression that hung over him like a dark cloud. Through grief counseling, he discovered that he was virtually disabled by the all-consuming disappointment he felt over the fact that his wife's illness had destroyed all the plans they'd made for their retirement years. Not only were many of their plans and dreams interrupted, he was now facing life alone, and in debt for her final expenses.

Regardless of the situation in which we find ourselves, if we want to move on, we have to take responsibility for our own emotional, spiritual, and physical well-being. By failing to acknowledge our feelings, or by blaming others for our pain, we only delay the healing process.

When we allow our feelings to be dominated by a sense of regret—perhaps the most agonizing and paralyzing of all emotions—we only intensify the anguish we already feel at our loss. When a mate dies, regrets often plague the one left behind. Eric put it well when he told me, "While death and divorce cause some similar feelings, there isn't a possibility of any resolution or reconciliation in this life when a mate dies. Death is the final arbiter."

Maybe we never got to say good-bye, or we wonder if our loved one really knew how much we loved him or her. Feelings of relief, that the ordeal has finally ended, may leave the survivor with a sense of guilt. Then there is the disappointment of interrupted plans or uncompleted goals.

The tendency to speak only in the most kindly terms about the deceased may invalidate old wounds or unresolved issues. We have to know that it's okay to acknowledge our feelings about the one who died, even if some of these are negative feelings. No relationship is perfect.

Widows and widowers who tend to remember only the best, and even embellish the characteristics and virtues of the deceased, can set up unrealistically high standards for any future relationships.

In the case of divorce, regrets may burden both parties, the one leaving the relationship as well as the one left behind. Whether or not to proceed with a divorce is an agonizing decision. It's especially difficult for members of the Church—regardless of the circumstances—and no one makes that choice without some remorse. The effects of that decision are widespread and profound.

To be divorced by one's mate is a devastating experience. It's an experience that certainly demands fierce determination and monumental effort, if the one left behind is to achieve a recovery of self-esteem and personal dignity. The impact of divorce may even be magnified if the marriage was solemnized in the temple.

Some make the decision to divorce and then wonder endlessly if it was the correct choice. Some singles, even those who had been the divorcing partner, said that they occasionally experienced "warm and fuzzy" feelings toward the former mate, and then wondered if they'd done the right thing. And many of these people had come out of horrible relationships! They allowed themselves to forget all about the problems and behaviors that led to the breakup, even accepting blame themselves where none should exist.

Perhaps these kinds of feelings and doubts come as the result of failure to separate reality from the illusions about our former spouses that we created for ourselves, as we struggled to make the relationship survive. We attribute qualities to that person that existed only in our hearts and minds. It might also be one of the reasons for some of the disastrous remarriages of previously divorced couples.

Little rituals have always been part of my life, so after much thought I decided to have a funeral for my pain and my anger. I'd make it a real funeral, with a casket and prayers and everything. I picked a Saturday a few weeks in the future and made no other plans for the entire day. By the time it rolled around, I was mentally prepared and ready to get it done!

It was a hard day.

I began by rereading the journal I'd been keeping since I'd made the decision to separate from my husband of twenty-six years. I paced the kitchen floor and sometimes talked to myself, but I purged all my pent up emotions. Each bit of anger, the sense of betrayal, and every one of the regrets. I also granted forgiveness to myself for my own failings in my marriage, as well as for each of the wrongs committed against me, and eventually I felt that I'd gotten it all out.

Over the course of the morning, I wrote down my thoughts on little slips of paper—I trapped every one of them. By doing this, I felt that none of it could ever come back to haunt me. Then I took all those little pieces of sorrow and pain and disappointment, and I placed them in a shoebox casket that I tied shut very securely with string. Prayerfully explaining my purposes to the Lord and asking his blessing upon my efforts, I went into the backyard, dug a hole, and buried all the bad feelings.

For me, this day marked the end of my old life and signaled the true beginning of my future. It was the end of the anguish of a broken marriage and the beginning of a long-sought-after peace of body, mind, and spirit.

Perhaps it sounds overly dramatic or silly to you, but this worked for me. Try to find something that will work for you. All the pain associated with the loss of a love can't stay bottled up inside without causing severe damage.

There is another kind of healing that may be needed, a healing of the spirit. If there are any other significant personal problems that have not been addressed previously, deal with them now. Don't wait. Unresolved problems—particularly those affecting our spiritual nature and membership in the Church—must be dealt with before a true and complete healing can take place or new growth can occur.

We need to remember that our children also need to heal from their loss, even adult children. Whether a parent has died or there's been a divorce, children will go through the same grief process. Their feelings must be acknowledged and dealt with, or they too will suffer undue emotional hardships in the future.

If at present you are so emotionally disabled that you can't assist them, please obtain outside support so someone will be there for them too. If private counseling is not an option, LDS Family Services or a grief support group might be another alternative.

Lots of us make mistakes along the way, especially when we're going through an ordeal that shatters our self-image or devastates us emotionally. Part of the growth we can experience during this period in our lives comes about as a result of looking at ourselves and then determining who we want to be from now on.

When we face our pain, refuse to compromise eternal principles, and place ourselves completely at the mercy of God, our righteous desires will be granted. And he will heal our broken hearts, if we let him.

It is imperative that our wounds be identified and healed before we attempt another relationship. Whether you've lost your mate through death or divorce, there are bound to be some emotional scars. Don't carry these forward to influence your future life. Leave the anguish behind, and be willing to receive the happiness and blessings that the Lord has reserved for those who love him.

Chapter 6

Starting Over

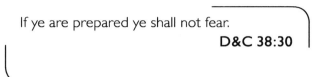

If ye are prepared ye shall not fear.

D&C 38:30

Jack, a thirty-eight-year-old whose ex-wife had custody of their two children, was reeling for months after his divorce, feeling as if he were spiraling out of control. He was terribly lonely and had difficulty managing his children's visits. Because of his work schedule, he hadn't actually spent very much one-on-one time with his kids, so he was on new ground there. He wasn't able to concentrate at work and feared his job might be in jeopardy. He was struggling financially even though he'd taken on a part-time job in addition to his regular employment. And he was tired!

In many areas, Jack had no options, but he knew he had to get a better handle on those things over which he did have some control. And he had to do it quickly.

If he were to come through the challenges that lay before him—and come through in good shape—Jack realized he had to refocus and gain some new direction for his life. And he knew that he couldn't do all this alone. He'd have to arrange some type of new support system for himself.

As newly single persons, we are in charge of our own lives. Of course, that power will never be absolute. There will always be outside influences that are beyond our power to control, but that's true whether we're married or single. We have to live with these, but there are lots of other things that we *can* control.

Maybe you've experienced some of the same feelings as Jack had and now you have resolved to take charge of your situation too. You've resolved not to allow feelings of helplessness and despair to make you a victim of the situation. You want to move forward on a path that will take you where you want to go in life and in the eternities. You've decided to get through the tough stuff, set new goals, and do all that you can to make your transition successful.

By making these choices, you've empowered yourself and are ready to seriously set about the business of building a new life for yourself.

Now you need to make a plan. A good place to begin is by determining your current needs.

You are the best person to assess what your needs are right now, but those close to you might have some valuable insights that you can't see. So it might be beneficial to involve people whose opinions you value around you.

This is a major undertaking and will influence everything you do. So, you'll need to do it thoughtfully and prayerfully.

You might start by listing your needs on a piece of paper, under categories such as temporal, physical, emotional, social, professional, financial, and spiritual. You might think of other classifications, but let's consider just these for now.

Temporal Needs: Do you have a safe place to live? Do you have utility service and a telephone so you can get help in an emergency or look for a job? Do you have dependable transportation? Do you have enough food? Do you have reliable child care?

Physical Needs: Are you experiencing any health issues? Are you taking good care of yourself? Are you supposed to be taking any medications that you've stopped taking? Are you eating well? Are you getting enough rest? Are you getting some exercise to reduce some of your stress? Are you keeping up your appearance? Is your weight putting your overall health at risk?

Emotional Needs: Are you depressed? Do you cry easily and often? Do you feel suicidal? Are you angry—like you might explode at someone and perhaps do them physical harm? Do you have someone to talk to who is a good listener? Someone who will set you straight if you get yourself off course? Are you using your solitary times for productive thought and reflection? Have you checked out the various support groups that are available? Are you eligible for social security or military benefits?

Social Needs: Are you alone a lot of the time? Are you shunning the friendly advances of coworkers or other people who care about you? Are you feeling sorry for yourself? Do you have someone to do things with? Are there certain times that are especially difficult for you to be alone? Are you participating in community or Church activities? Are you nurturing your relationships with your family, friends, and coworkers? Do some changes need to occur?

Professional Needs: How are you doing at your job? Has your emotional state affected your performance? Is your employment in jeopardy? Do you need to get a job? Do you need to brush up on rusty skills or take special training to make you more employable? Are you networking to increase your prospects? Do you have the clothes you need to work? Do you have you transportation to and from your job?

Financial Needs: Do you know how much income you have coming in after taxes and other deductions? Do you own property? Do you have any investments? Do you know how much you owe, what it's for, the terms of repayment, and the interest rates? Do you own extra vehicles or have too much furniture? If money is short, can some of these be liquidated to generate cash?

Spiritual Needs: How is your testimony? Is it strong, or is it a little shaky right now? Are you having personal prayer and reading scriptures and other gospel-related materials each day? Do you have a calling? Do you have a home teacher you can count on? Are you serving your visiting teaching sisters or home teaching families? Do you need more instruction in gospel principles? Are you paying your tithing? Is your temple recommend current, and are you attending the temple regularly? Are your activities maximizing your opportunities to receive the inspiration of the Holy Ghost? What more can you do?

As you review the answers to questions like these, your list of needs will become the basis for the new support system you can build to help fulfill those needs.

Some of the solutions will come from things you can do and changes you can make. For example, Sundays were always my undoing. I managed to get through each week fairly well, but at the end of the meetings, when everyone went home with their families to a good dinner, I went home to an empty house that screamed its silence at me. I dreaded Sundays because I was so lonely—and it was so easy to feel sorry for myself.

Planning ahead—anticipating times such as Sundays and holidays—helped me avoid finding myself in a funk. Involving others usually guaranteed that we could all avoid the doldrums!

When it's something that's not possible or practical to handle by yourself, support will have to come from those you enlist to help. Try not to overlook anyone or anything that might assist you in overcoming the challenges you're facing right now. And make certain that everyone is on board and understands exactly what help you need. For example, if you're going to sign up for an Institute class every Thursday evening, and you need a babysitter, make sure that Aunt Sally understands that it's once a week, on Thursdays, for six weeks. Then be certain that you're punctual. People usually don't mind helping out, but they don't want to feel taken advantage of, so be considerate. If someone turns you down, recruit someone else.

The Church can also play a role in providing support for newly single individuals by helping us retain an eternal perspective on all that's happening in our lives, reminding us of things we already know but may in our distress have forgotten, overlooked, or abandoned. Like having regular prayer, gospel study, and giving service.

The friendship and concern of other members of the Church can fortify us until we are strong enough again to stand alone. And priesthood blessings and administrations can give solace when it seems that nothing else can. But the Church can only fulfill its role if we let it, and if we make our needs known to those who have stewardship over us.

Along with determining your needs, you need to clarify your vision of the future. Scrutinize all the different segments of your life and see how well each part is going to accommodate your needs and contribute to the accomplishment of your goals.

Don't forget to include things that make life satisfying, enjoyable, and fun. Are there interests you haven't pursued for a long time? Is there a long-buried passion that you now have time to resurrect? Want to join a bike club? Take a painting class? Participate in musical theater? What have you got to look forward to? Have you seen your extended family in a while? Been to a class reunion? Had a massage? Gone to Know Your Religion lectures or the Family History Center lately?

The people around us can enhance our lives. Some will be new acquaintances, whereas other friendships may simply need refreshing and a little tender loving care. Some of the people in your life are strong, so you can lean upon them, and others may be delicate and sensitive, themselves requiring care and compassion. There will be people who provide beauty, inspiration, and examples you can follow, while others will bring you laughter and joy.

When we make our faith and determination to live the gospel to the very best of our ability the foundation for all our planning, we've chosen the protection of the gospel and unifying influence of the Church. Then lots of difficulties and choices resolve themselves. We simply need to remain steadfast and count our blessings!

The Father of our spirits has built worlds without end and constructed numberless universes that man hasn't even discovered yet. With such divine parentage, surely we can muster the fortitude and summon the faith and courage to rebuild our lives.

Remember the words of Alma: "I am weak . . . [but] in his strength I can do all things" (Alma 26:12).

As Latter-day Saints, we know who we are and that we possess knowledge and power granted us from on high. We are the recipients of promises, the likes of which our mortal minds cannot conceive.

If you could imagine your ideal life, how would that look? Remember that the kind of life you end up with will be determined by how you live from day to day. The goals you set now, the values you embrace, the direction you go in, and the qualities and characteristics you include in your new persona as a single person will help to take you there.

As plans are formed, our expectations must be realistic if we are to avoid being crushed by repeated disappointments. Our previous expectations—those things we had looked forward to, hoped for, and had confidence would occur in our future—are going to have to change now that we're single again. But that doesn't mean that we can't have hope in the future, things to look forward to, or plans we'll enjoy bringing to fruition. They will just be different than the expectations we had when we still had a mate.

Part of the good that can come out of our experience, as newly single individuals, can be the pleasure of exploring and uncovering all that life has in store for us in our new circumstance. With this exercise, this planning process, we're just getting some of the wrapping off the present!

Chapter 7

Look Before You Leap

> A man travels the world over in search of
> what he needs, and returns home to find it.
>
> **G. Moore**

If there is ever a time when we need the influence of the Spirit, it's during this transition from being married to becoming single.

To most of us, this is a scary time. The future can seem so uncertain. All the things that gave stability and predictability to our lives may have been badly shaken or perhaps completely destroyed.

You're probably facing a lot of major decisions right now. However, you might want to give some thought to just maintaining the status quo for a while. There are going to be a lot of new feelings to get used to, new situations to cope with, and extra demands upon your emotions, resources, and time. Maybe it would be better for now to just wait and revisit some of these choices in a month, or three months, or next year.

Too many changes, all at once, only create more stress. Maybe it would be better to eliminate as much pressure as you can by deferring some of the really life-changing decisions until some of the smaller issues are resolved. Decisions made during emotionally charged times sometimes turn out badly. But once made, these can be hard or even impossible to retract.

Maybe you feel inclined to leave the home you occupied while circumstances related to your current situation were still going on? Does moving into another house or apartment really seem like a good idea, if you take your emotions out of it? Perhaps, instead of moving to new living quarters, it might help to simply sleep in a different bedroom.

Where we live, our surroundings, and our possessions can provide a sense of security and comfort—unless our home has been the scene of something terrible, in which case it might be a good idea to make a change.

Perhaps you're in a job that previously seemed less than what you feel you're capable of, and maybe you've even been looking or sending out feelers. But think about this for a moment. There can be a lot of comfort in doing a job that we know well, one that we can perform without a great deal of anxiety, even if the professional challenge or the pay seems less than we needed before. It can also be comforting to be around people who understand our current situation, eliminating the need to explain why we look haggard and don't laugh much or why the kids call at work so often. The familiar can be reassuring. A job change can sometimes wait.

Prior to her decision to separate, Karen had been thinking about changing jobs, but after a lot of thought and prayer, she abandoned that idea in favor of staying where she was to avoid the added stress inherent in undertaking a new position. The support of her coworkers during those months of adjustment and confusion was a blessing. They were like an extended family, staying in the background but always there for her if she needed them. Several months after her divorce, Karen decided that a change of scene would be good for her, and she sought out a job that would take her out of state. By then, Karen felt ready to venture out on her own into a new environment.

If the time comes when we are ready to admit that we want to get married again, we need to carefully and honestly examine our reasons. We need to ask ourselves early on—before we become emotionally involved—why we want to get married. What are the motivating factors?

Just as we analyzed our needs in building our support system, we need to determine the reasons we want to marry again, and—whether we desire marriage for the wrong reasons. And we need to identify those feelings that might cloud our ability to be objective.

Marriage is not a cure for existing problems. The excitement and romance at the beginning only alleviates our problems for a little while; then they reappear, exacerbated by the addition of a new spouse and perhaps even additional children.

It's especially important for divorced singles to reflect upon the difficulties in the prior marriage to determine the root causes of the breakup. Consider whether these issues have really been resolved or if it's likely these factors tagging along could taint a new romance.

The importance of resolving issues—before becoming involved with someone—can be critical to the success of another relationship. More about this later.

One of the most difficult parts of planning for a new future is anticipating pitfalls. My dictionary describes a pitfall as an unsuspected snare, danger, or drawback. And, in the life of a newly single person, there can be many!

Recognize your vulnerability and guard against making life-changing choices until you're sure you can anticipate all the consequences of those decisions. Many changes and decisions can be postponed with few, if any, consequences, but there are many that can be difficult to undo. For those of us starting over single, it might be better to err on the side of caution.

Chapter 8
Money Matters

I will . . . open you the windows of heaven, and pour you out a blessing.

MALACHI 3:10

There might be some newly single individuals for whom finances are not an issue or a concern. If that's you, you have permission to skip this chapter and go directly to the next chapter.

For the rest of us, the loss of a mate has an almost immediate impact on our finances. While I am admittedly far from being an expert on finance, I'd still like to toss out some ideas, options, and alternatives for your consideration. Some of these may prove helpful or might inspire you to come up with some brand-new notions.

There is an amazing key to financial management available to each of us. That key is the payment of tithing. And the more pressing our needs, the more urgently we need to live this financial law of the Lord. The stories associated with payment of tithing are numerous, but let me share a few with you.

As a newly baptized member of the Church, I was convinced that if we paid 10 percent of our meager income as a tithe, our family of six would starve and we'd lose our home. Nevertheless, we agreed that we needed to do this. With the encouragement of our bishop, and a promise of help from the bishops' storehouse if the cupboards did indeed become bare, we wrote the first tithing check.

As you might guess, our food never ran out, all the bills were paid, and over the next several months, our income increased dramatically. As long as we were faithful in paying our tithes and offerings, we had everything we needed.

I am also convinced that the payment of tithes was responsible for some of the spiritual guidance I received as a newly single person and for solutions to some of my financial difficulties that seemed to come out of the blue.

Those of us who have tested that commandment have gained fervent testimonies of the blessings that come from paying tithes and other offerings to the Lord. If it is a gospel principle you've not yet come to trust and appreciate, I encourage you to make it a matter of prayer. Ask that you might be granted the faith to live this spiritual law, because that's what it takes. Not money, but faith—to trust in the Lord's promise when he says, "Prove me," and see what happens.

That could be the conclusion of this chapter, the perfect solution to financial woes, but there is also a practical side to coming to grips with money matters.

Unfortunately, when the primary wage earner (usually the man) is no longer contributing, the widow or divorcée may be confronted with an almost immediate need to find a more affordable home. Men, facing child support or alimony payments, are often required to quickly locate relatively inexpensive accommodations, since income must be stretched to support two households.

The increased demand for senior missionary couples could provide a solution to the need for affordable housing as it did for me. If you are available and can obtain some references, let it be known in several of the surrounding wards or stakes that you'd consider house-sitting. Ask lots of questions and come to some kind of agreement that can be put into writing and signed by both you and the homeowner. Misunderstandings can abound if the arrangement is not very clearly stated.

Another alternative is home sharing. Two or more people go together as roommates to rent a home or apartment and then split the expenses. This could also provide an answer to child care, if the only employment option involves working a swing or graveyard shift.

If you fear being alone or get depressed without someone to talk to, a roommate might be a good choice. And again, expectations should be well defined and in writing. Renting a room with kitchen privileges is another option that provides companionship.

There are also people who are willing, for a variety of reasons, to take someone into their home. For example, an elderly or disabled person who needs additional income or is just lonely and doesn't want to be alone at night.

Just because your home has always been a house or an apartment you occupied with your spouse, and possibly your children, doesn't mean that you can't be happy in some other situation. Brainstorm! Get some friends to assist you in thinking of some other alternatives, and then pray for guidance and inspiration to help you find an appropriate solution.

Another financial consequence of becoming single can require that insurance coverage be rearranged. You may lose the multiple driver discount on your automobile insurance, which may increase the premium on your vehicle. But dropping coverage should not be an option. Life, disability, and health insurance mustn't be overlooked either. If you don't now have this coverage, and need to obtain employment or change jobs, look for an employer with benefits that include low- or no-cost coverage. Try to negotiate having it start right away.

Homeowner's insurance is frequently included in the mortgage payment, so some of us don't even give it a thought. If your situation demands that you rent, check into renter's insurance to protect your liability and whatever possessions you bring to your new home. The property owner does not insure your belongings! This insurance is relatively inexpensive, especially in relation to the potential of loss if a catastrophe occurs.

Wherever you live, find a way to protect yourself financially. Most of us have no way to replace furnishings lost, for example, in a fire or earthquake. Neither have we the resources to defend ourselves against a lawsuit or to pay a settlement for a liability claim if someone were to slip and fall on our sidewalk.

Utility costs (and property taxes) can be significant and can strain the resources of those of us already on a tight budget. Some companies and agencies have provisions for individuals with special circumstances. There is no charge to find out if you can qualify for some relief in either of these areas, so ask!

We've been talking about things that require us to spend money, but what if there isn't any money right away to spend on insurance premiums, rent deposits, and so forth? Let me share a few thoughts about this from my own experience, along with those of some friends who were also in rather dire financial straits.

When I separated from my ex-husband, the $138 from my half of the cleaning-deposit refund on our apartment didn't go very far. I was netting less than $800 a month after taxes, and among other things, I needed to pay six months in advance to get automobile insurance in my own name. I needed over $200, and I just didn't have it. But I *did* have a nice water bed stored in the garage. I spread the word that it was available and quickly obtained a buyer. I was able to make the insurance payment and had enough left over for an oil change on my old car.

This experience led me to reevaluate my other material resources. Because I was house-sitting, I wouldn't really need my share of the furniture for at least another year, so I decided to convert what I had to cash. I hoped it would take care of the more pressing financial needs that I was facing. Over the next several weeks, I went through everything, determined fair prices, and sold the lot.

Friends asked me how I could do that. How could I let go of the things that were dear to me? It was simple: I needed the money more than I needed those things.

Carol went through a devastating experience when she lost her husband of over forty years in a terrible auto accident. He had always handled all their financial affairs, and in the process of settling his estate, she discovered that they were deeply in debt. Although she had a teaching degree, Carol hadn't worked in years, remaining at home to raise their now-grown children. There was an insurance settlement, but it wasn't enough to cover all they owed to creditors after her living expenses for the next few months were taken out.

She realized very quickly that she'd have to sell her home and relocate to something much smaller, since there was not sufficient income to cover the rather large mortgage payment on the home they'd recently built, plus the insurance and property taxes.

Carefully, and with a great deal of sorrow, Carol separated out those items she could take with her to a small condominium. Proceeds from the sale of miscellaneous items, excess furniture, and appliances carried her through until the home was sold.

The equity from the sale of her home was sufficient to enable her to make a substantial down payment on a small condo, and left her with a comfortable monthly payment she'd be able to handle. The rest went to the creditors. It was very hard, but she was a real trooper. She did what was necessary and never looked back.

One of the amazing parts of her financial story was the amount of money generated by her yard sale. She went though everything, pulled out all of the duplicates and items that had lain unused in drawers and boxes for years. Her son helped her identify and price her husband's tools and fishing paraphernalia. She even put small, related items together in zip-lock bags—things I probably would have just tossed into the trash. Things like embroidery floss, scraps of ribbon, hair rollers, and small kitchen gadgets were bagged together and offered for fifty cents to a dollar per package. She tagged everything clearly and put up signs around the neighborhood, and over two sunny afternoons she sold almost all of it—and made over three thousand dollars!

Never underestimate the earning potential of a well-planned yard sale. When money is scarce and needs are pressing, sometimes we have to get creative to come up with ways to generate funds.

Some of us inherit financial obligations that can seem overwhelming, and we wonder how we'll ever be able to pay them off. In this case, it might be beneficial to work with a credit-counseling agency. These nonprofit organizations often provide free budgeting workshops and counseling, along with debt-management programs to help individuals avoid bankruptcy. After working out a strict budget with you, they contact creditors to arrange reductions in interest charges and, perhaps, extensions of the time allowed to pay off the debt. Creditors are usually happy to accommodate these arrangements since it means that they will eventually get paid. When someone files bankruptcy, the creditors usually get nothing.

Low-income single mothers entering or reentering the workforce are sometimes deterred in their job search by lack of a professional wardrobe. They feel they must accept low-paying, menial jobs, such as fast-food restaurants. While their skills (or ability to learn quickly) may be sufficient to qualify for a higher-paying position, they are reluctant to even try. They're afraid they don't have the right clothes for that environment. But there are ways to get around this.

In virtually any community there can be found at least one resale shop. Such shops take clothing, shoes, and accessories on consignment from individuals, including well-to-do professionals.

Here's how this works. The consignors purchased high-quality, fashionable, name-brand merchandise and then either outgrow or tire of it. They place nearly-new garments for sale in a consignment shop, where they can at least get some money back. Only merchandise that has been freshly laundered or dry-cleaned, is in current style, and in like-new condition is accepted. Some items are even brand-new, still bearing the original store tags. Prices usually run about 20 to 60 percent of the retail value, and most shops will even do layaway. The owner of the shop usually takes 40 to 60 percent of the selling price and pays the difference to the owner of the consigned garment. After a certain period, if the item hasn't sold, the prices are generally cut in half. Part of the fun here is that you can be both a buyer and a seller (which is very helpful if your weight changes rapidly).

These are just a few ways to raise or save money, and you can probably come up with several more. Let your imagination soar! Let go of any preconceived notions and you might be surprised at the financial resources you'll discover.

Your credit rating is another area that may be new to you. Some women have never had credit in their own names. As a result, it may be difficult to obtain credit for urgent needs that simply cannot be paid for in cash right away, such as emergency auto repairs, replacing a critical home appliance or furnace, or purchasing a car.

You need to know the good or bad news about your credit standing as soon as possible. To wait to establish credit in your own name until a pressing need arises could be disastrous. To obtain a credit report, contact a credit reporting agency. There may be more than one in your area, and each might include different information. Be sure to ask for a report in your own name only.

Credit reporting agencies are required by law to provide you with a copy of your report if you've been refused credit. Ask the company that turns you down for the name of the reporting agency, then contact them and tell them that you were declined.

Once you get the report, go over it carefully. Phone for explanations or see someone at your financial institution to help you interpret the data if you find it difficult to understand. If you find errors in the information, call the agency and ask how you can correct the mistakes. It's your right to include explanations in your file, and the agency is required to convey these comments to prospective creditors.

If your credit rating is good, hurray for you! If it's not, or if there is simply no information on you, then you'll have some work to do.

Let's talk about how to establish a good credit rating. To enable a potential lender or creditor to assess what kind of credit risk you will be, they have to see a record of your credit transactions. If you have no experience, establishing a credit history on your own will require that you purchase something on credit or borrow some money and then repay it according to the specific terms of the contract. For this purpose, it is not to your advantage to pay anything off early. Creditors want to see a pattern of payments made on time over an extended period.

If you do need to establish credit in your own name, one very conservative way might be to borrow money from yourself, the suggestion offered to me by the manager of my bank.

This is how it worked: The bank issued me a loan of five hundred dollars at an interest rate of 8 percent for twelve months. I immediately deposited the entire amount in an interest-bearing savings account at 6 percent for a net interest cost of only 2 percent.

I'd intended to make regular withdrawals to cover the payments, but as it turned out, I got a raise almost equal to the amount I needed each month. At the end of the year, I still had the five hundred dollars, and I had a credit record!

Establishing a good credit rating can also be accomplished by buying one or two smaller items on credit. A new set of tires for two hundred dollars, paid for over the course of one year, for example. The important thing is to make the payments *on time* for the *full period* of the contract.

Remember, this is a special tactic for a specific purpose; it's not carte blanche to run up a bunch of charge purchases.

An attractive financial peril can frequently be found in our mailboxes: preapproved credit cards. When money is short and needs are pressing, the temptation to accept these offers can be difficult to resist, especially when we're depressed, because buying things usually makes us feel good. However, this is never the answer.

This may seem like a contradiction after our discussion about establishing a credit history. But one involves controlled purchasing to obtain specific long-term benefits, and the other results in uncontrolled spending that could lead to financial disaster. Self-discipline must be exercised where the use of a credit card is concerned.

We've talked about how there may be no way to make our incomes stretch as far as (perhaps) two paychecks used to go. How you manage will, of course, depend on your particular circumstances; but let's look at one more area that deals with money: savings.

An old sage said the problem of how to save money affects only those who think they have no money to save. A possible answer to this dilemma could lie in the wise counsel I received during a temple preparation class taught by the stake patriarch.

In our payment of tithing, the patriarch explained, we are merely giving back to the Lord what is already his. Heavenly Father allows us to use 90 percent and only asks for 10 percent in exchange for all that he has given us.

We perform labor in exchange for pay in order to provide for our temporal needs during our sojourn on earth. Most of us pay our 10 percent to the Lord off the top, he continued, and then we pay the rest of our income to our creditors. In this context, he said, our creditors include the mortgage holder on our home or our landlord; the grocer; the electric, gas, and water companies; the auto manufacturer; and so forth. In the end, we actually work for nothing—because we fail to pay ourselves!

What he said was true. I had never, in my entire life, "paid" myself. The patriarch explained that as long as we were faithful and honest with the Lord, our needs would be taken care of. Further, he explained, the secret to what he called financial security is in paying the Lord first, then paying yourself a similar amount, and living on the balance.

Have you the courage and faith to put this principle to the test? We're told that paying tithing takes faith, not money. Perhaps it also takes faith in ourselves, to pay ourselves for the work we do.

Managing our finances as newly single individuals can be challenging, even a bit overwhelming, but we can make it if we work as if our success depends entirely upon our own efforts, and pray like it all depends on the Lord.

I developed the following budget plan for myself when I was single. It helped me, and I hope these ideas will be of value to you.

Chapter 9

A Simple Budget Plan

> The mint makes it first; it is up to you to make it last.
>
> EVAN ESAR

Money Management and Record Keeping for Non-Bookkeepers

Motto: Impulse is out; planning is in.

Purpose:

- take charge of personal funds through controlled spending
- increase awareness of where money is going
- forecast needs and eliminate impulse purchases
- encourage systematic saving
- pay obligations on time

Overview

This is a simple system. Don't be intimidated because you see a bunch of forms. These are to help you get started as you identify

- who you have to pay and whether you're paying interest
- why you need to pay it
- when it's due
- amount to be paid (or an estimate)
- whether to pay by cash or check or electronically
- which paycheck you want to use to pay for each item in your budget

Once you begin to use your plan, you'll quickly develop a record of where your money's going, and that will help you make adjustments to your spending habits and plan ahead so you don't get caught short when a bill suddenly shows up.

Here's how this budget plan works:

In **Step 1** you'll complete a Budget Planning Worksheet that will help you identify everything you spend money on—not just your housing expenses and debts, but everything! The worksheet will guide you in deciding whether to pay cash, write a check or money order, or to save ahead. By using this worksheet, you need the money on hand when it comes time to purchase or pay for an item.

"Save ahead" means that you'll have to anticipate an amount you'll owe or will be spending—on Christmas, for example. Divide by the number of months until you'll need the money. That's how much you need to save on a regular basis.

Here are some examples of Save-Ahead funds and how to calculate the amounts.

Insurance premiums: Divide the amount of the premium by the number of months or pay periods until the premium is due. For example, if you will owe $240 in six months for auto insurance, divide the $240 by six. This means that each month you will need to save $40 in the Save-Ahead Insurance Fund.

Medical: If you anticipate that your out-of-pocket expenses for the year will be $120, then save $10 each month in your Save-Ahead Medical Fund.

Christmas gifts: Divide the total amount you plan to spend by the number of months left until you'll need the money. If it's January, for example, divide the total by twelve; if it's June, divide the total by six. Then deposit that amount each month into your Save-Ahead Gift Fund.

Clothing: Go through your wardrobe; list items you really need and when you must purchase them. Plan ahead for sales. Buy winter things in spring, summer things in the early fall, shoes in February and August, household items at pre-inventory clearances, and so forth.

Auto maintenance: List routine needs such as lube, oil, and filter changes, wheel rotation and balancing, tune-ups, brake alignments, and other anticipated major repairs (watch for coupons in the newspaper). Determine the total for the next year and divide by twelve.

The tighter your budget, the more important it is to plan for routine maintenance on your vehicle to avoid major repairs. Watch fluid levels, keep the battery cables free of corrosion by cleaning with a wire brush, keep the oil clean to protect engine against unnecessary wear. Ladies, ask male friends for the name of a good mechanic or auto shop, then talk to each until you find someone you feel will give you good advice. Have them give you a list of regular maintenance items, how often you need to perform them, and what the approximate cost will be.

Each month these amounts should be placed in the Save-Ahead Fund. Place cash in your Petty Cash Keeper, in slots or envelopes that correspond with each particular cash budget. Whenever you buy something, you'll pay cash and then put that receipt in the particular fund's envelope, to replace the cash spent. Use cash for items for which a check is either impractical or unnecessary, like movies, coin-operated laundry machines, or gas for your car.

Each Budget Period—the time frames that correspond with your income dates (for example, the fifth and twenty-fifth of the each month, if that's when you get paid)—you'll take out the receipts, record the information about your cash purchases in the "actual" columns of your budget record, and file away the receipts for future reference. Then, in the pay period you've determined for that fund, you'll replace the cash you spent, bringing your Cash Fund back up to your budget amount.

The total in the Petty Cash Fund is always the same. Whenever money is spent, the fund is reimbursed, back up to the total amount. At any time, the sum of the cash, plus the receipts, should equal the total amount of the budget for that fund.

One reason to set up a Petty Cash Fund is to help you become aware of every amount you spend. This will help you discipline yourself and keep on your budget. If you've come to the point where you're working through this exercise, then you've committed yourself to doing better financially. By doing so, you've promised yourself that you'll not spend more than you've allowed each pay period for your cash needs, and that when your Cash Fund in a specific category is spent, you won't borrow from another fund unless it's an emergency.

You'll write checks (or money orders) for items requiring proof of payment, or that have to be sent through the mail. Money is deposited into the checking account equal to the amount needed to cover checks and bank charges for that period. If a minimum balance is required to eliminate bank charges, try to maintain that balance. It might be a good idea to leave this amount out of the balance showing in your check register.

Each pay period, you'll deposit the amount you budgeted for personal savings and to save ahead. You'll keep a record of the total in your savings account as personal savings and by your Save-Ahead Funds earmarked for specific future expenses, such as insurance premiums, clothing, anticipated travel, auto maintenance, gifts, and medical copayments.

You'll deposit savings into one or two savings accounts (whichever you choose) and then record those amounts in a notebook to keep track of the purpose of every dollar in savings.

You can set up as many different funds as you need. You'll distribute the total amount of your deposit to the savings account among the various funds according to your budget plan.

Example of Tracking Savings

If in the current pay period your savings and Save-Ahead budget amount is $116, in your tracking book you'll mark that $25 went to personal savings, $62 to the insurance account, $15 to the medical account, $10 to the Christmas Fund, and $4 to magazine subscriptions. Then you'll figure the new balances in each fund and bring those totals down to the last line.

When items you've saved ahead for become due, you'll withdraw from savings the exact amount (for a quarterly insurance premium, for example) and deposit that money into the checking account to cover the check you'll be writing to the insurance company. Likewise, when you buy an article of clothing or renew a subscription, you'll take the money out of that savings fund and deposit it into checking, to cover the amount of the check that you wrote.

Note: Personal savings might be kept in a separate savings account if the bank's fees are low and you'd rather not mingle your save-ahead money with personal savings. If you have an IRA or other investments, money from savings might be transferred by phone, wire-transfer, or online to those accounts. Check with your financial advisor.

Please stop now and take a few minutes to look at the following example worksheets and forms. Then come back and continue.

Completing the Budget Planning Worksheet

You need:

+ A Cash Keeper—a small file such as a coupon or canceled check file
+ A personal checking account (or money orders)
+ A savings account(s)
+ A notebook with columns, a spreadsheet program or word processor to recreate the example charts, or enlarged photocopies of the blank forms following the example worksheets. You may also email the author at ceoinc@cableone.net with "Budget Forms" as the subject. Please specify if you prefer Excel or Word formatting.
+ A small spiral-bound pad (at least 4–5 inches wide)

Step 1: Set up your Budget Planning Worksheet so the column headings match the example.

+ List everything you spend money on and all of your financial obligations, regardless of how small or insignificant each may seem, along with the dollar amount you spend (or think you spend) for each item.
+ Determine your payment method for each item in the budget. This means whether you'll use cash, check, money order, debit, or credit, or if you need to save ahead each pay period to have enough money when it's time to actually make the payment.
+ Determine the frequency with which each item is to be funded. How often will you need to replenish each budget item?
+ Determine the due date for each item. Decide which pay period each item will be funded from and mark it on the worksheet.
+ Include each long-term expense item that you need to pay at some future date, and the amounts you need to save each pay period, in your Save-Ahead Fund so you'll have enough.

Step 2: Now you're ready to set up your budget trackers for each pay period. Set up one form if your income arrives monthly, two if twice per month or every other week, four if you get paid every week.

Using information gathered in Step 1, set up your budget trackers for each pay period by filling out the appropriate spaces. See the examples for January 15th and January 31st.

Step 3: As you pay bills during each budget period, write in what you spent. This will give you a clue down the road about those items and amounts you need to change. If you have budgeted $50 a month for telephone, but you regularly spend $65–$70, you need to change your budget. If your income is not high enough to give you a lot of flexibility, you'll need to reduce some other budget amounts to offset the increase to your telephone expense, unless you can cut down on telephone usage.

Step 4: At the end of each budget period, reconcile the amounts you spent or paid against your plan, and include the over- or under-budgeted amounts, plus the transfers you've made from savings (for save-ahead items) to checking.

Other dollar stretchers:

- Use coupons for auto maintenance, groceries, nonfood items, dry cleaning, restaurants, and entertainment.
- Plan menus around seasonal availability and sales and use a list when you grocery shop.
- Look for day-old items at reduced prices (such as bread and meats).
- See movies on dollar night, use coupons, or go to second-run theaters.
- Ask if your bank or credit union offers coupons for anything you need.
- Attend dress rehearsals of concerts, plays, and other performances; these tickets are usually only a few dollars.
- Make your newspaper subscription count by clipping coupons from the Sunday edition.
- Consign like-new clothing you can no longer wear to a resale store.
- Use the public library rather than purchasing books and magazines.
- Sell off excess furniture, tools, clothing, and so forth to raise money.
- Find a way to market your hobbies, or teach a class about your hobby to pay for supplies.
- Car pool! Take the bus, bike, or walk to work.
- Turn down the thermostat and put on a sweater in fall and winter.

- Wash dishes by hand to save water. Only use the dishwasher when you have a big load; same for laundry.
- Find something to earn extra money. You could pay bills and balance checkbooks for busy or elderly persons; help people write family histories; take cans or newspapers to the recycler for cash; house- or pet-sit; plant spring flowers or clean up garden remnants for a busy homeowner; or do personal shopping for a busy executive.
- Talk to other singles about ways they have found to save money.
- Make do or do without.
- Learn to distinguish between your wants and your needs.

Sample Savings Account Register/Tracker

Date	Savings	Insurance	Medical	Clothes	Auto	Balance
12-31-06 Balance forward						983
12-31-06	500	122	55	225	81	
1-15-07	150	12	35		15	1195
1-12-07				Smog sticker	−12	1183
1-15-07	Renter's ins.	−62				1121
1-17-07		Dr. Jones	−15			1106
1-31-07	150	24		75		1355
1-28-07			sweater	−21		1334
Month end bal.	800	96	75	279	84	1334
2-15-07 Balance forward						1334
2-15-07	150	12	35		15	1546
2-28-07	150	24		75		1795

Sample Budget Planning Worksheet
Step 1: Determine method of payment, frequency, and amount

Method: C = Cash, K = Check, S = Save					Budget Monthly Amount		
Method	Budget Item	Frequency	Budget Amount	Due Date	Cash	Check	Save
K	Tithing	½–2X	300	1, 15		300	
S	Savings—personal	½–2X	300	1, 15			300
K	Rent—roommate	M	350	1		350	
K	Electric	M	50	15		50	
K	Heat/gas	M	50	15		50	
K	Phone and Internet	M	25	15		25	
C	Food	½–2X	300	1, 15	300		
C	Nonfood Items	½–2X	30	1, 15	30		
C	Auto gas and oil	½–2X	50	1, 15	50		
S	Auto maintenance	M	15	15			15
K	Maintenance/repairs	—	Actual				From savings
C	Dry cleaning and laundry	—	24	1, 15	24		
K	Car payment	M	150	15		150	
S	Auto insurance	M	24	1			24
S	Renter's insurance	M	12	15			12
K	Insurance premiums	Q	Actual				From savings
K	Life insurance	M	38	15		38	
K	Credit card	M	25	15		25	
K	Student loan	M	75	1		75	
S	Medical expenses	M	35	15			35
K	Copays and Rx	—	Actual				From savings
K	United Way	M	10	15		10	Auto ded.
C	Entertainment	½–2X	50	1, 15	50		
S	Clothing	M	75	1			75
K	Clothing purchases	—	Actual				From savings
C	Newspaper	M	11	15	11		
C	Postage stamps	M	7	1	7		
K	Bank charges	M	5	1		5	Auto ded.
C	Miscellaneous	M	40	15	40		
TOTALS			2051		512	1078	461

Frequency key: W=weekly, 2X=bimonthly, M=monthly, Q=quarterly, A=annually, —=as needed

Sample Budget Tracker

For the Income Period Ending January 15, 2007 (Step 2A)

Method: C = Cash, K = Check, S = Save		Actual	Actual	Actual Amounts Paid/Used (Step 3)				
Method	**Budget Item**	**Budget Amount**	**+ / (−) Budget**	**Cash**	**Save**	**Check**	**Check #**	**Date Paid**
K	Tithing	150				150.00	1658	1-10
S	Savings—personal	150			150			
K	Electric	50	(7.41)			42.59	1659	1-10
K	Heat/gas	50	14.85			64.85	1660	1-10
K	Phone and Internet	25	(1.50)			23.50	1661	1-12
C	Food	150		150				
C	Nonfood items	15		15				
C	Auto gas and oil	25		25				
S	Auto maintenance	15			15			
K	Maintenance/repairs	Actual				12.00	1662	1-12
C	Dry cleaning and laundry	12		12				
K	Car payment	150				150.00	1663	1-15
S	Auto insurance							
S	Renter's insurance	12			12			
K	Insurance premiums	Actual				62.00	1657	1-5
K	Life insurance	38				38.00	1664	1-15
K	Credit card	25				25.00	1665	1-15
K	Student loan							
S	Medical expenses	35			35			
K	Copays and Rx	Actual				15.00	1666	1-15
K	United Way	10			Auto ded.	10.00		
C	Entertainment	25		25				
K	Clothing purchases	Actual			From savings			
C	Newspaper	18		18				
C	Miscellaneous	40		40				
TOTALS		995	(5.94)	285	212	592.94	1089.94	
		Budget Amount	**Over (Under)**	**Cash**	**Save**	**Check**	**F**	
		A	B	C	D	E	C+D+E= F	

Reconciliation

Regular Amount to Pay Budgeted Items				= A	995.00
Transfers	**From Savings**	**To Checking**	**Step 4**		
Jan.–Jun. HO Ins.	(62)	74	From Savings	= G	94.94
Dr. Jones Copay	(15)	15	Total Paid Out	= H	1089.94
Total Transferred	G	89	Add down: A + G = H − H must = F		

Sample Budget Tracker

For the Income Period Ending January 31, 2007 (Step 2B)

Method: C = Cash, K = Check, S = Save			Actual	Actual Amounts Paid/Used (Step 3)				
Method	**Budget Item**	**Budget Amount**	**+ / − Budget**	**Cash**	**Save**	**Check**	**Check #**	**Date Paid**
K	Tithing	150				150	1667	1-19
S	Savings—personal	150			150			
K	Electric	350				350	1668	1-20
K	Heat/gas							
K	Phone and Internet							
C	Food	150		150				
C	Nonfood items	15		15				
C	Auto gas and oil	25		25				
S	Auto maintenance							
C	Maintenance/repairs	12		12				
K	Dry cleaning and laundry							
S	Car payment	24			24			
S	Auto insurance							
K	Renter's insurance							
K	Insurance premiums							
K	Life insurance	75				75	1669	1-20
S	Credit card							
K	Student loan							
K	Medical expenses							
C	Copays and Rx	25		25				
S	United Way	75			75			
K	Entertainment	Actual				21	1670	1-25
C	Clothing purchases							
K	Newspaper	5			Auto ded.	5		
C	Miscellaneous							
TOTALS		1056	0	227	249	601		1077
		Budget Amount	Over/ Under	Cash	Save	Check		F
		A	B	C	D	E		C+D+E=F

Reconciliation

Regular Amount to Pay Budgeted Items				= A	1056.00
Transfers	**(From savings)**	**To checking**	**Step 4**		
Black sweater	(21.00)	21.00	Over/Under Budget	= B	
			From Savings	= G	21.00
			Total Paid Out	= H	1077.00
Total Transferred	G	21.00	Add Down: A+B+G=H; H=F		

Budget Planning Worksheet
Step 1. Move funds from Savings to Checking as needed.
Purpose: to determine method of payment, frequency, and amount.

Method: C = Cash, K = Check, S = Save					Budget Monthly Amount		
Method	Budget Item	Frequency	Budget Amount	Due Date	Cash	Check	Save
TOTALS							

Frequency key: W=weekly, 2X=bimonthly, M=monthly, Q=quarterly, A=annually, —=as needed

Sample Budget Tracker

For the Income Period Ending _____ **Step 2** ___

Method: C = Cash, K = Check, S = Save		Budget Amount	Actual +/(−) Budget	Actual Amounts Paid/Used (Step 3)				
Method	**Budget Item**	**Budget Amount**	**+ / (−) Budget**	**Cash**	**Save**	**Check**	**Check #**	**Date Paid**
TOTALS								
							F	
		A	B	C	D	E	C+D+E= F	

Reconciliation

Regular Amount to Pay Budgeted Items				= A	
Transfers	**From Savings**	**To Checking**	**Step 4**		
Jan.–Jun. HO Ins.			From Savings	= G	
Dr. Jones Copay			Total Paid Out	= H	
Total Transferred			Add down: A + G = H − H must = F		

Chapter 10

Someone to Watch Over You

Man hath two attendant angels ever waiting
by his side.

JOHN CRITCHLEY PRINCE

Among the most important people in the lives of newly single Saints can be good and faithful visiting and home teachers.

Who can better recognize and understand the utter devastation of a man who has just lost his wife than another man? Home teachers are faithful priesthood holders who know the family, are familiar with the circumstances, and have a divine stewardship for that man.

Who could provide a more compassionate heart, sympathetic ear, or better sounding board than the visiting teachers who have been there throughout another sister's ordeal? And could there ever be a more critical time for a priesthood presence in a home than when a woman has lost her husband? Home teachers can fill that important need and bring the comfort and assurance that only a priesthood blessing can provide.

Regardless of the cause of the loss of a spouse, the result is the same. Someone who had a wife or husband is now alone.

The home and visiting teaching programs of the Church are divinely inspired to provide friendship and support that is more personal and intimate than most of the casual Church associations we enjoy with one another. Home and visiting teachers carry the mantle of stewardship for the souls under their charge. Our home teachers are our conduits to the bishop, who has at his disposal many additional Church resources that might be used for our benefit in trying times.

If we think back on it, virtually all answers to our prayers have been brought to pass through the hands of someone else. As we struggle through our difficulties—whether it be the grief and loneliness of a mate's death or the commotion and devastation of divorce—we can receive comfort and strength from those whom God has appointed to look after us: our home teachers and visiting teachers. But only if we let them into our lives.

Check in regularly with your bishop. Let him know about your situation, whatever it might be, and keep him informed about any changes taking place in your life. Seek his counsel on major decisions, and avoid those places and situations that might later require you to tear down and rebuild sections of your life.

As Latter-day Saints, too many of us are well practiced in putting on a good front. We go to church and smile. "Yes, we're doing just fine, thank you," we say. We may keep a stiff upper lip but then go home and cry.

If there were ever a time when we need to be real, this is it. There's no disgrace in admitting that we're hurting or in asking for a little extra help. By so doing, the blessings have a chance to go two ways: to us as the recipient and to those who provide for our needs as the givers.

When we're working through a personal loss, we need all the blessings we can get. That's why it's also important that we take especially good care of those in *our* charge, even though we may not be feeling very charitable at the moment. We need to keep on serving, because giving service is one of the best ways to overcome self-pity and depression. It takes us out of ourselves and gets us thinking beyond our own immediate problems.

If you've been faithful in this area, remain so now! If you've been lax, repent, serve the brothers or sisters in your area, and set a goal to be willing and loyal in the future. Ask for an assignment if you don't have one, and watch the faces of your leaders light up! You just made someone's day.

Home and visiting teachers can provide a unique source of help and comfort in our time of need, and we can return that favor as we watch over those whom we are called to teach.

As members of the Church, we recognize and sustain the presidents of the Church as prophets, seers, and revelators appointed as the Lord's mouthpiece to the world. As such, we regard their instructions to us as divine. So, that makes the counsel to reserve Monday evenings for family home evening a direction from our Heavenly Father. Remember the promise from Doctrine and Covenants 82:10: "I, the Lord, am bound when ye do what I say."

Having children in the home provides a good reminder to the mother or father who now heads the family alone. We've also been told that even if the family consists of only a single individual, we should still have family home evening.

It is no doubt a poignant experience to conduct family home evening in the absence of the mate who either took charge or helped with those Monday evening activities. It is an area where his or her absence will be conspicuous, but this could provide a special opportunity for recalling happy occasions and sharing feelings.

Home teachers and their families could be invited to participate in family home evening in the beginning, perhaps to act as facilitators to draw children out and help bridge the transition.

A structured environment might benefit children by helping them to feel comfortable expressing their feelings, especially if these include anger, guilt, or disappointment. Family home evening could provide a vehicle to help them move through the stages of grief. Children also sometimes put on a happy face to protect the feelings of the present parent.

Devoting some time to talking about the family's situation and the events surrounding the changes in the family might open the way for children to talk about things that otherwise might be internalized.

The thought of holding family home evening can be more than a bit disconcerting for those who live alone. What are we supposed to do? Read a lesson out loud to ourselves? Sing "We Are All Enlisted"? Make a pan of brownies and eat the whole thing by ourselves? Why bother, anyway? After all, "Do you have family home evening each Monday?" is not one of the questions on the temple recommend interview, right?

Monday evenings could be very rewarding for singles. It could provide a specific time for reading the scriptures and reflecting on gospel principles, catching up on all those back issues of the *Ensign*, working on family history or genealogy projects, organizing and assembling photo albums, or maintaining contact with extended family members.

People who live alone or single parents sometimes forget to make special times for themselves to do things they really enjoy. We often become so task oriented, or try to keep busy to avoid thinking too much, that we fail to remember the simple pleasures that can be associated with doing things just because we want to or because they make us feel good.

Joining forces with another member who's also alone or including another single-parent family for family home evening might be a good way to initiate this activity, or even to lend some variety to the usual Monday evening.

Each time we keep a commandment or strive to accomplish something we've been counseled to do, we reap the blessings that are contingent upon that act of obedience. That promise is guaranteed because it is based upon eternal laws. Couldn't you use a few more blessings?

Chapter 11
Personal Assets

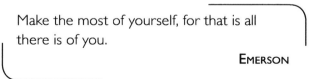

Make the most of yourself, for that is all
there is of you.

EMERSON

As singles, most of us will find ourselves becoming part of a larger circle of acquaintances than when we had partners. We want to be accepted in our new situation. We'd like others to seek out and enjoy our companionship, and we want to take pleasure in theirs. We want to be included as part of a new group of peers, even though, given a choice, we might prefer that it not be *this* particular group.

Our new social status provides yet another opportunity to take further charge of our lives, build social confidence, and enhance our self-esteem. So far, we've talked about self-improvement in many areas, but now we're going to get really personal. We're going to look at becoming an individual with lots of personal appeal. Someone that other people—men and women, singles and married folks—will want to be around.

This period of transition can provide not only the opportunity, but also the motivation and incentive to get ourselves into better shape physically, as well as emotionally and spiritually. We're not talking about those early morning aerobic shows on TV. What we're talking about is a natural extension of efforts that may have already been set in motion in other areas of our lives.

It's hard to feel down in the dumps when you feel good about yourself. There is a special sense of well-being when we know that we're working hard to be the very best that we can be, and that we're succeeding.

Once again, the starting point is an evaluation, but this time it begins with your personal assets—those things that are great about you.

Most of us have a difficult time acknowledging the good things about ourselves. Many of us were taught not to be conceited, and that making a positive statement about ourselves is bragging. But did you ever read any self-deprecating statements made by the Savior? Of course not! His statements in reference to himself were always truthful and always positive. This was not evidence of personal pride; he knew who he was and what he was capable of doing and being. He could never have accomplished all he did if he had used the same kind of negative head-talk we put into our minds. We need to be more like him in this way.

None of us are perfect physical specimens, but we each have attractive qualities on which we can capitalize to increase our overall appeal. There is no shame in admitting our personal merits. You know if you have a great smile or an infectious laugh. You know if you have good posture and a firm handshake, that you can quickly put others at ease, or that you're a good listener. Start a list!

If you're not sure or you're just too modest and self-effacing to do this for yourself, ask someone to help you. Ask several people. Explain what you're doing—trying to develop your positive attributes—and request that they tell you what they like or admire about you on a personal level. Either way, add all your appealing qualities to your list. We're talking about evaluating all your assets as an individual, and then figuring out how to maximize and build upon these so you can improve your overall attractiveness and increase your confidence and self-esteem.

Please remember: we're not talking about how well we fit into some ridiculous media-driven ideal. We're talking about appeal that goes beyond physical appearances. We all know people who have flaws in their appearance, yet they don't let these seeming imperfections stand in the way of their self-image—or their striving for success. (Nor do most of us give these a thought when we're admiring them.)

Take the actor John Goodman, for example; he has what we refer to as a "weight problem." World-famous model Lauren Hutton has a large gap between her front teeth. Audrey Hepburn was thin as a rail and had virtually no shape. Abraham Lincoln had terrible posture. The renowned physicist Stephen W. Hawking is wheelchair bound. At fourteen, Joseph Smith was, according to some folks, too young and lacked the formal education to be believable. Prophets Moses and Enoch were both "slow of speech" (Exodus 4:10; Moses 6:31). And of Jesus Christ it was written, "He hath no form nor comeliness; and . . . no beauty that we should desire him" (Isaiah 53:2).

Sometimes we don't allow ourselves to see past those things we consider our own deficiencies. We tell ourselves we have nothing to offer, people don't like us, or we can't compete with those who are younger or older, thinner or fatter, prettier or more handsome, better educated, funnier, more talented, blah, blah, blah, blah!

Why do we do this to ourselves?

Elizabeth used food to assuage the anger and frustration she felt over problems in her marriage. Her weight had increased gradually until finally she had gained over eighty pounds. When she got divorced, her husband laughed when he told her that she was old (she was just over forty), fat, and wore glasses and that no other man would ever look at her. At the time, she believed him.

Once the stress of the relationship ended, her weight seemed to fall off with little effort on her part. Her sparkling smile and the new light in her eyes took years off her appearance. Several months after their separation, when their paths accidentally crossed, he didn't recognize her. And when he finally did, she said the look on his face confirmed to her that the transformation her friends had been exclaiming over had truly taken place. She decided that her newfound happiness and confidence were the best revenge.

Starting over single can include a new resolve about working toward a more healthy weight—whether that's a gain or a loss. Incorporating regular exercise will improve not only our appearance, but how we feel. It's difficult to feel strong when we're physically frail or weak.

Several months after losing her husband of over forty years, the appearance of my sweet sixty-seven-year-old neighbor declined dramatically. Each time I saw her, Marge looked thinner and seemed to have aged more. Her whole countenance seemed withered.

I worried about her for months, but she seemed so fragile, I didn't want to say anything. Then one sunny afternoon we met while retrieving our mail, and she looked positively radiant! I couldn't restrain my surprise, much to her delight. She explained that she'd been shopping at the mall with her daughter, who had dragged her kicking and screaming into one of those cosmetic stores that do makeovers. This insightful daughter, seeing her beautiful mother beginning to fade away, had taken action, and the result was amazing. The change in her physical appearance had dramatically affected Marge's mood and her outlook. She hadn't realized how far she'd withdrawn into herself.

When we're emotionally down, we can quickly lose interest in how we look. Every time we see ourselves, how we look sends a message to our minds that we really do feel horrible! It can be a vicious cycle. Men let their hair grow out or may not bother to trim facial hair (or nose or ear hair). Women don't bother keeping up their perms or their nails. The same dull clothes are worn, day after day. Even bathing can become a chore that seems more than we can endure, so it might be skipped.

And until we do something, or someone lovingly forces us, to break out of that cycle, it can hold us captive. Loss of interest in our appearance is one of the first signs of depression, a clinical condition that can often be treated with medication.

Seeing herself with a little makeup again and her hair fixed restored to my lovely neighbor the belief that her life was not over, life was good, and the future could still offer happiness. Not the same happiness she knew with her sweetheart of so many years, but new, different kinds of joy.

Marge moved away about a year later to be closer to her grandchildren, but I heard she had married again and was traveling the world with her new husband, a retired history professor.

These two success stories are offered to remind you that good things can and do happen to those who have the courage to strive for something more. We get comfortable with who we are.

Changing ourselves—especially our physical appearance—can be a little scary. People notice! It calls attention to us, but so what? What's the worst possible thing that could happen if you show up looking a little different? Chances are that those who know and care about you will be delighted and will fall all over themselves telling you how great you look.

Speaking of new looks, as part of your personal inventory, how about taking a look in your closet? How long has it been since you've had some new duds? Do you guys still have a polyester leisure suit hanging in there? Or ties showing remnants of the meal you ate when you last wore it? Ladies, when was the last time you wore something bright? Something with a little pizzazz? Red, yellow, or how about a nice bright blue?

If your budget is tight, reread the earlier chapter where we discussed resale clothing shops. Maybe a fresh cleaning will do. Laundering and ironing a garment with a little starch or sizing could work wonders.

This brings up a potentially sensitive subject: personal grooming.

The most frequent complaint among the single sisters about the men at church dances seemed to be (sorry, gentlemen!) body odor. They could forgive unironed shirts and mismatched colors, but they had a hard time tolerating close proximity, especially when too much aftershave was added to the other . . . problem. This was enough to discourage a lot of the women from coming back to the dances after a time or two.

Sometimes we fail to notice our own peculiarities or idiosyncrasies, but if we want to be accepted by others, we might have to put ourselves in their place and take a good look at ourselves. When we are nervous (the probable cause for what we just talked about) or we get excited, many of us exhibit signs of stress. Some of us sweat; others develop a little laugh that follows everything we say, making us sound a little silly. Others withdraw into a shell and appear aloof and unapproachable. Some of us are gum-chewers; the tenser we become, the more we beat that poor gum to death.

Someone once said, try to see yourself as others see you—but try not to get angry about it. When Karen first began going to single adult functions, her children insisted that it was time for her to get a new hairstyle. They complained that as long as they could remember, she'd worn the same look, the one they called the helmet. With the help of a friend, Karen made a change, and it made her feel absolutely giddy!

Later she worked up the nerve to ask a trusted friend to observe her in various circumstances, and then report back to her on his observations. It revealed a number of things she felt she could improve upon, and it was a great help.

Bradley was intimidated by walking into a crowded room where he didn't know anyone, but everyone there seemed to know one another. As a result, he tried to appear confident, which a friend told him, only made him appear aloof and kind of mad—the opposite of what he wanted.

Reducing the chances that we are going to inadvertently undermine our own efforts to be more socially acceptable will build our confidence that we can meet new social situations well. That, in turn, will increase our desire to participate.

Unfortunately, first impressions are frequently lasting. This goes for our personal appearance and the appearance of our possessions and surroundings. Look at your home and your vehicle, and to try to see these through another's eyes.

If your place could use a little TLC, now might be a good time to give it a going over from the inside out. Cleaning out drawers and closets will give you a perfect opportunity to take inventory of your clothes and other belongings. Get rid of what you no longer use, and shine up what you do.

A very wise man once said, "Stop accumulating: everything you collect means just another thing for you to keep clean." After everything is sparkling clean, keep it that way by doing a twenty-minute pick-up each evening before you turn in. A twenty-minute pick-up is a brief sweep through the house to put things back where they belong, straighten up the pillows on the sofa, take out the old newspapers, and so forth. This allows you to wake up to a nice, neat home, which can set the tone for the rest of your day.

When you offer a ride to a friend, do you apologize for the mess inside your car? Are you carrying around six months' worth of empty soda cans and fast-food wrappers?

When I was growing up, whenever my father went out to work on the Chesapeake Bay oyster boats, I stayed with a neighbor woman who lived down the road. In that part of southern New Jersey, almost everyone was poor. Lacking a mother at home, I was quite the ragamuffin, until Auntie (as everyone called her) got hold of me. She also boarded foster youngsters for the state and was a proud, dignified woman despite her apparent poverty. Her motto, stressed to us children repeatedly, was how important it was to be clean and neat. And every day she scrubbed us until our faces shone, just like the toes of our shoes! It didn't matter that we were poor and our clothes were old and a bit threadbare; they were clean and mended, she said, and we should stand tall and hold our heads up. Sage advice, even today.

Taking charge on a very personal level, being honest with ourselves, and making a sustained effort toward self-improvement builds self-esteem. The Lord said, "Mine house is a house of order" (D&C 132:8). When the clutter and chaos around us are replaced by calmness and confidence, our minds can be more open to receive the inspiration of the Holy Ghost.

The Lord has said, "Men are, that they might have joy" (2 Nephi 2:25). The knowledge of our true identity—spirit children of heavenly parentage, occupying earthly tabernacles—can bring not only joy, but also an unspeakable sense of gratitude for the love and blessings that are ours.

Reflected in our countenance, that joy can be the most magnetic personal attribute one can possess, setting up an irresistible attraction to which others are drawn. And it can provide a light and an example to our brothers and sisters who languish in the gloom of their own difficulties.

People are attracted to happy, confident individuals. That kind of appeal has little to do with our size or shape, what we do for a living, or what kind of car we drive. But it has everything to do with our reflection: letting the light of the gospel shine forth from our whole being, as one who has overcome their trials by faith.

Here's one final thought to sum up all we've talked about and provide a perfect formula for success in this effort:

Marcus Aurelius said: "Be thyself."
Socrates said: "Know thyself."
Jesus said: "Give thyself."[1]

Source Notes

1. George Bickerstaff, *So Well Expressed* (Salt Lake City: Bookcraft Publishers, 1964), 82.

Chapter 12
Socializing Again

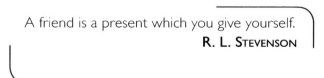

A friend is a present which you give yourself.
R. L. Stevenson

The prospect of going out socially again can be both exciting and frightening. Dating, at this point in our life, can't be approached the same way we did it in our youth. After we've been married, we are very familiar with how to be a wife or a husband, but usually we've forgotten how to behave as a date. There's a big difference.

We're still dealing with a close relationship with a member of the opposite sex, just as in our marriage, but the ground rules have changed dramatically. Dating again can be fun and exhilarating, but after having been married, it can also present some real challenges. This is one reason it's probably best to first get your feet wet through the Church's single adult functions.

Other challenges facing those starting over as single (often middle-aged) adults include overcoming shyness, lack of people in our own age group, and bewilderment over how to get started in the dating game again. The Internet is becoming a tool for singles who cope with these obstacles. Type "LDS singles" into your search engine and watch as dozens of websites pop up. I know many happy couples, including family members and Church friends, who met this way and who found it to be a comfortable way to test the waters from a safe distance, allowing them to get to know someone before meeting face to face. Use caution, however. Ask other singles who have used the Internet to meet LDS singles, and find out about their experiences, both good and bad. Then decide for yourself whether it is something that might work for you.

The Church sponsors gospel-centered activities designed to entertain, educate, uplift, encourage, and inspire us. At the same time, these activities remind us that we're children of God who are on a path to exultation, a fact that may easily become muddled when we're vulnerable. When we begin to venture out socially, most of us can be comfortable in group settings geared to our special circumstances, such as firesides and single adult conferences. You'll hear many of the same concepts and counsel you find in other church meetings, but reminders never hurt.

When a relationship ends, the love we used to give to our mate doesn't depart with them. It's usually still there, except now we have no one on whom to bestow it. Church-sponsored recreational activities for single adults—dances, picnics, dinners, sports outings, and the like—are another great place to begin venturing out socially. That love we used to give to one special person can still be given away, only in smaller portions and to a variety of people. It's one of the ways to help heal the hurts and to fill the void.

Lots of newly single people think they will never want to date again, let alone remarry. But most of us eventually give in to our inherent need for social contact, affection, and love. Our divine nature leads us to form close relationships. Most of us do better in a committed relationship. Married people are happier, healthier, and often live longer than their unmarried counterparts.

A friend told me about a gravely ill man who called his wife to his side when he knew the end was near. Tenderly he expressed his great love for her, his tearful appreciation for all they had shared through the years, and his gratitude for all she had done to make his life joyous and full. Then he told her that the greatest compliment she could pay him, after he was gone, was to marry again. This, he explained, would demonstrate that she, too, had valued and enjoyed the relationship they'd shared—so much so, that she would desire to have that special association again. He asked her to promise that if a proper opportunity presented itself, she would marry again. What a wonderful, loving gift he left his widow!

If you listen carefully to your heart, you'll know when you're ready to seek outside companionship. Don't let others push you into it before you feel ready. And by the same token, don't allow anyone to hold you back. Our need for companionship is divinely appointed and there is no element of disloyalty in finding happiness again.

We can participate in Church single adult activities not for the express purpose of finding a mate but for self-development, increased spirituality, and friendships with peers of both sexes. The peer support available there, and the opportunity to learn and benefit from others' experiences, is immeasurable. But the benefits we derive from our participation will depend greatly upon how much effort we are willing to expend, not only in our own behalf, but also in behalf of our brothers and sisters in the program. Each of us has some personal responsibility to help make the Church's efforts successful.

The common denominator that each of us needs to remember is that every one of us is a child of God, beloved of our Heavenly Father. Each person has something unique to offer, if we are willing to take the time and trouble to get to know him or her. And we have something to extend to them—a warm smile, a friendly greeting, and a sincere inquiry regarding their well-being. In other words, we can share ourselves without regard to station or status.

No one questions the right of anyone to attend Church-sponsored activities. No one asks at the door if it's appropriate for us to be there. All are admitted and as long as they deport themselves well, no one is asked to leave. This policy has its good points, but it also lends itself to some disadvantages.

In some areas the single adult program has a less than flattering reputation. Frankly, a lot of members won't participate in many of the activities. The reasons are varied, but let me share some of my own observations made over the two and a half years I participated.

This special group of people represent a virtual microcosm of humanity: there are the bright and the beautiful, the poorly educated and the plain, the happy and the seriously depressed. There are the well-to-do and the poor, younger people and senior citizens, the talented and the handicapped. There are the fastidious and, as we discussed before, there are those whose grooming leaves much to be desired. Some have never been married, while others have been married several times. (And some are still married but think it's okay to attend single adult socials while waiting for their divorce to become final, which is definitely not the case.)

Most participants are good members of the Church, but occasionally unscrupulous individuals have been known to pass themselves off as members in good standing—in order to prey upon vulnerable, inexperienced singles. We would like to believe that Church activities are safe havens, but we must remember to be alert and cautious, just as we should be under any other circumstances. Latter-day Saints tend to be very trusting, and this can lead to some sad situations. Use reasonable caution and don't assume goodness.

Is that reason to stay away? Of course not. But it is good reason to keep our wits about us. Just remember that anyone who suggests anything that conflicts with the standards of the Church should be avoided—and probably reported to someone in authority, so the person can be checked out.

When you meet someone at a single adult activity, use the same good judgment to evaluate him or her as you would use if you met someone on a public bus or while picking up your dry cleaning. In other words, use your head, trust your instincts, and don't be fooled by *where* you meet someone.

Almost without exception, the people you meet through Church single adult functions will be just like you—a little self-conscious, a bit awkward, and quite hopeful about making a good impression.

Like you, they want companionship. They like to be listened to and find others to whom they can relate. They hope to have a little fun or gain some inspiration and strength to help them make it through the next few days or weeks.

The Church-sponsored single adult activities present many opportunities to build new relationships. If we try not to prejudge the people we run into, giving everyone the same chance we'd like to be given, then participating in these activities can enhance our efforts to find healing and happiness.

Listen to everyone's story; pick out his or her mistakes and see if these also belong to you. Some of us have been in relationships that leave us a little bitter, and mingling with others whose values and goals are like our own is a good way to rediscover the fact that all men and all women are not alike.

As we mingled together at single adult functions I attended, we had some wonderful conversations as we share stories about our lives, our problems, and our aspirations. Most of us felt free to really open up since we were all in much the same boat. We laughed until we cried, and we consoled one another, gave advice, offered support, and often felt like one big extended family. It was through these conversations that I learned so much about how previously married people feel about their situations, what they did and didn't like about their status, and what they saw as the advantages and disadvantages of participation in Church-sponsored activities—and what each gender did and didn't like about the other.

Now, I've already told the brethren about the sisters' chief complaint seemed to be. Now it's your turn, sisters, to find out about the men's major criticism of the single women.

The most common complaint among the brethren was that so often the ladies seem needy. They said many of the sisters looked forlorn or sad, as if they were just waiting for some nice man to come over and *make* them happy. The men were unanimous in their declaration that women who seemed confident and looked happy were the most attractive. (Please notice that there was no stipulation about weight, age, or other appearance issues.)

No one wants to feel responsible for another person's happiness. That goes for both men and women. Don't sit around like a lump with a long face, thinking that if you look woeful enough someone will feel sorry for you and come over to cheer you up. It probably won't happen. Don't harp on your tale of woe. Remember that happy people are attractive people.

Do we need to wait for the Church to have an activity, or to come up with a new phase of the single adult program for us to get together to have some fun? There are lots of things to do and lots of people to do them with if we take a little thoughtful initiative. Have fun—at Church-sponsored activities and on your own.

When you're ready to expand your socializing beyond the realm of firesides and Church dances, where else can you go for other group activities? Believe it or not, there are lots of alternatives to bars. For example, try music groups, college or community choirs or instrumental groups, local theater groups, sports leagues, book clubs, computer-users groups, garden clubs, political or special interest groups, community volunteer programs, college and community education classes, or part-time employment (if you're retired) in a job where you meet the public. Go ahead and add to this list. Go where you're likely to find the type of people you enjoy. Find your passion and pursue it, and along the way you'll surely meet new friends.

From this foundation of group pursuits, it's easier to move on to one-on-one relationships. A good way to start having dates—but with less pressure—might be to begin by going dutch. Drive your own car, meet somewhere neutral, and pay your own way.

You might purchase discount movie tickets and let your date spring for Chinese food (a good, inexpensive dinner about equal to the cost of the theater tickets). If this goes well—and you feel mutually attracted and share enough common interests—you might venture out on some real dates.

The ongoing intimacy of the marriage relationship results in certain automatic responses between the sexes. This puts singles between a rock and a hard place: there's temptation if we pursue one-on-one relationships, and there's loneliness with the probability that we'll never find another mate if we don't. The apostle Paul put this succinctly in his letter to the Galatians: "For the flesh lusteth against the Spirit, and the spirit against the flesh: and these are contrary the one to the other: so that ye cannot do the things that ye would" (Galatians 5:17).

While we're still getting ready for real dating, it's probably the time to do what my teenagers used to call "the seminary drill." That's when you make decisions and rehearse how to handle situations beforehand. By setting dating standards once, you never have to make those decisions again. If we don't do something like this, we could find ourselves in big trouble.

The old adage "one thing leads to another" is true, especially where single men and women are concerned. This isn't the format for a sermon on morality, but there are four points I'd like to touch upon in the context of this discussion.

One basic difference between most men and women is that men often give affection for perhaps no other reason than it feels good to cuddle or they think it's expected. Women, on the other hand, often mistake those demonstrations of affection for deep interest or even love.

Many sisters have at one time or another experienced some real deflation because of misconstruing the motivations of gentlemen friends. Couples kiss, maybe cuddle, and share some warm fuzzy moments. He goes home, not giving the encounter too much thought; she's there thinking he must be falling for her. And the seeds of disappointment are planted.

Brethren, be clear about your intentions. Sisters, don't attach deep meanings to what may only be intended as friendly gestures.

Sexual relations are not sanctioned outside of marriage. That statement is a no-brainer for most of us, but experience prompts me to include it, nevertheless. I've interviewed many single adults and LDS counselors who work them. As a result, I heard several tragic tales of individuals to whom this statement came too late. Naive members had been seduced with the argument that as long as sexual intercourse doesn't take place, or if the activities are between members of the Church, it's okay.

It's *not* okay.

If any doubt or confusion exists in your mind, get clarification from your bishop and let him recommend some authoritative reading materials.

Sisters and brethren, do not attempt to validate your self-worth with sex. This is an especially treacherous pitfall just waiting for the unsuspecting. When our egos have been battered, and our self-image distorted by negative relationships, we are so hungry for approval and confirmation of our appeal that both men and women can be extremely vulnerable to seduction.

We cannot—indeed, must not—measure our individual worth through the actions or behaviors of another person. Insecure, emotionally shattered women especially can fall prey to this type of unscrupulous manipulation more easily than might be anticipated.

If we choose to date people who are not members of the Church, we need to remember that as Latter-day Saints our standards of behavior may not be the same as theirs. It's not to say these people are not moral individuals; as Latter-day Saints, we may hold ourselves to a higher law than our friends who are not members of the Church.

Dating again can be fun and exciting, but after having been married, it can also present some real challenges. But dating is necessary, for how else can we find someone with whom to share the rest of our lives?

It's funny—that thing about finding another someone to love. So often it's when we least expect it that "the one" shows up. Maybe it's because when we're not looking, and we really relax about wanting someone in our life, that we become the most attractive. We've finally gotten to a place where we're happy with ourselves and with our life and not feeling desperate. Somehow that condition, that self-assured, tranquil state of being, attracts others like bears to honey!

The best advice for me about prospecting for a marriage partner came from a speaker at a single adult fireside. He said not to set out on a search for Mr. or Ms. Right. He counseled us to simply prepare for the mate we desired, so we will be ready when he or she comes along.

Chapter 13

Committing Again

> The supreme happiness of life is the conviction that we are loved.
>
> VICTOR HUGO

There are many previously wed singles for whom the longing to be married again can be relentless, overwhelming, and in some cases, nearly emotionally disabling.

The reasons for this are diverse and vary in intensity. Some of us liked being married and want to experience it again. Some depended heavily upon their mates for spiritual strength, and an even greater number (both women and men) for financial support. Those with children still at home may feel overcome by the burdens and strenuous demands of single parenting. Others feel lost without the association and companionship a mate provides. And the loss of physical intimacy—not only sex, but also the mutual affection that comes with being married—can be a real problem, but one that is rarely discussed, except in terms of cautious admonitions.

Many singles marry out of a desperate need to not be alone anymore, but that's not a good enough reason to marry. There are so many other things to consider before taking the plunge, especially the next time around.

Nationwide, the divorce rate for second marriages is even higher than the 50 percent of first marriages that fail. In my own area, where relatively few singles came out to activities, there were a surprising number of individuals who'd been married three or more times. Some had even remarried their former spouse and had been divorced again.

When we're recovering from the loss of a mate, whether by death or divorce, the heartbreak can linger and the effects can be long lasting. It's easy to fall in love to mitigate our pain and ease our loneliness. It provides quick but temporary relief from depression and poor self-esteem. We get this rush of euphoria, kind of like eating chocolate. Things that bothered, worried, and plagued us seem to disappear, and we feel wonderful. We greet each day with a smile, look better, and have more energy. Life is good—at least for the time being. But we shouldn't try to cure old wounds with a new marriage. We have to heal first from the inside.

If we've been single for a time, we also need to consider some of the advantages of being single that we'll be giving up. The opportunities and freedom you enjoy as a single will be restricted by virtue of the marriage. The longer one has been single, the more this factor might need to be weighed. This is where a review of the pros and cons of marrying versus remaining single might be of real value. (This sounds cold and analytical, but unless we reflect upon all the ramifications of remarrying and all the practical aspects, how can we be certain of our reasons and our readiness?)

Another question to contemplate is the question of what we expect to get from the new mate and the marriage. To every action and every behavior, there is a consequence of some kind—a cause and effect. We need to weigh the likelihood of those expectations being realized. Are our expectations realistic, or are we deluding ourselves?

This is a sensitive domain because it's often an area where objectivity is extremely difficult. If one has conscious expectations, they're relatively easy to validate. But if those expectations are rooted at a deeper level, it may take some work to uncover them. For example, a friend of mine fell in love and rather hastily married an energetic, well-to-do older man. While they never discussed it beforehand, she loved to travel and assumed that, since he was retired, they'd be seeing the world together. It was only after the marriage that she discovered his desire to settle down quietly close to his grown son's family so he could spend his time with his seven grandchildren. Each made assumptions about the other that were incorrect. Each had unspoken expectations that, if considered beforehand, probably would have influenced their decision to marry.

Expecting someone who's active in the Church to stay active is a reasonable expectation. But there are other, less obvious expectations that might take a little digging to uncover.

Almost a year after finishing my self-definition, I began to cautiously entertain the possibility of having another man in my life. I even went so far in my thinking as to allow that I might consider marriage again, if that opportunity should present itself. (That pushed me completely outside my comfort zone.) I seemed to drift naturally toward a certain type of male personality. Fortunately, I quickly saw that this would take me into a relationship just like the one I'd left.

Some of us wander aimlessly about, making acquaintances here and there, dating this one and that one—kind of like browsing through a shopping mall with a wallet full of money, wanting to buy something, but not knowing what we really want or need.

Remember how our mothers always told us to never go grocery shopping on an empty stomach and to always have a list to avoid impulse purchases?

That's still good advice, especially when it comes to considering a potential marriage partner. To make a wise choice, we do better if we know ahead of time what we want and don't want.

I started thinking about the consequences of continuing down the path I was on and determined that if I didn't want a repeat performance, I'd better figure out some alternatives. I got out the journal in which I was writing my self-definition and began a new section called "Qualities I desire in a mate and in a marriage relationship."

As I thought about this, day after day, I'd jot down thoughts and ideas as I'd done before, only this time it was about someone else—the man of my dreams, an imaginary man. I carefully considered every aspect of the personality of a man that I could love forever. I worked on it for several weeks and when it was finished, I read it every day, along with my own self-definition.

I believe it was because of this exercise that I recognized that man when I finally met him. He came in a little different wrapping than I'd imagined (as did I, for him) but it was definitely him. There was no doubt about it!

Everything about him fit the outline: his honesty and integrity, his loyalty, and his devotion to the Lord. I'd even speculated, under a section called "It would be really nice if . . ." that I'd like it if he played the piano or guitar or loved to sing. Well, he loves to sing and plays a little piano. And as they say, two out of three ain't bad!

If we don't know what we want, we won't be able to recognize him or her when that person comes along. We might overlook someone who could be the answer to our prayers—the love of our life!—because we never bother to look past age or weight or hair (or lack of it) or any of the dozens of other superficial judgments we tend to make about people.

And if we know what we *don't* want, it's more likely that we'll put a rapid end to a budding relationship that could turn out to be a disaster before we become too emotionally involved.

A new marriage may also involve blending two families. Sometimes too little consideration is given to this matter, and to the possible consequences of attempting to put together children whose life experiences may have been dramatically different. Blending families that include adult children can also be challenging.

Sometimes this effort works out marvelously well, but other times it's proved a catastrophe!

Whenever children are involved, it's crucial that open communication takes place beforehand and extraordinary consideration be given *before* the decision to join forces is made.

Discussions should include more than the topic of children. We also need to delve into specifics about our individual personal lives and styles. Consideration needs to be given to money management, sex, Church activity, tithes and offerings, recreation, shopping habits, plans for the future, retirement goals, temple service, serving a mission, financial needs and obligations to creditors, extended family, potential responsibility to aging parents or other disabled relatives, health conditions, and any other topics that might affect the marriage. Money and sex are listed at the beginning of this list because these two are cited most frequently among the issues causing marital conflicts and divorce.

All issues with the potential to influence and seriously affect a new union should be discussed frankly and honestly to determine, ahead of time, a couple's compatibility.

Now that we've brought up the subject of sex, let's talk about a couple of things—especially as it relates to new marriages.

While no one should marry again just for sex, neither should we underestimate the need and desire for intimate relations as a motivator in the decision to marry again. Nor should we fail to take into account that sexual problems from a previous union might come forward into a new union.

Many of these types of problems result from the simple lack of understanding on the part of *both* partners—with regard to the feelings and needs of the other. Let's look at some of the basic differences that must be given sensitive consideration by wives and husbands.

It's fairly well documented that the men's sex drive often exceeds that of most women. This difference often shows up after the initial excitement of a new marriage dies down and the doldrums and demands of everyday life drain some of the romance out of a marriage.

Asked to prioritize personal needs, most men will place sex very high on the list. Some women might place it somewhere after the need for chocolate, but before new shoes, or vice versa. Right off the bat, we may be dealing with some serious incompatibilities!

The expectations placed on many of today's women to be home-makers, mothers, and assistant breadwinners exacerbates the spread between men and women by placing enormous demands on her energy and stamina. While there is a more equitable division of household labors today than there was years ago, the primary responsibility for seeing that the house is clean, the cupboards are full, the meals are on the table, and that children are cared for still falls to the woman.

In addition, when the man is away from the home a lot (such as traveling for work or in performance of Church callings) she may also have to function as primary disciplinarian, taxi driver, bookkeeper, and in some instances, provide the spiritual stability for the whole tribe. In real life, she may have little or no time to even *think* about sex! (Behavioral scientists claim that the majority of men think about sex dozens of times each day.)

Too few men truly comprehend the overwhelming physical and emotional drains that can deplete or even totally wipe out a woman's sex drive. Asked how she feels, most of the time a woman's answer will be, "Tired." And she really is.

And in spite of a man's hinting, cajoling, and complaining, too few women truly understand the intensity of their husband's sex drive.

Each partner often erroneously assumes that the other's needs are the same, or at least believes they should be, as their own. When these differences are made known and considered, a satisfactory compromise can be usually worked out that will meet the needs of both.

Couples often experience great sex when they're on vacation alone together. They sleep in, have no deadlines or alarm clocks, and they have all the time in the world. They're both well rested and undistracted. They lose themselves in each other. Each wonders why it can't be like this all the time.

Sexual need can be compared with any other human appetite: it's there but it's different for each of us. Who among us would deny our partner food just because we're not hungry yet? And why should we scoff at the suggestion that a peanut butter and jelly sandwich sounds really good just because we had peanut butter and jelly sandwiches two or three weeks ago?

We adjust and compromise and make reasonable accommodations for our beloved in so many ways, so why not where lovemaking is concerned? Why can't we lovingly allow and provide for each other's differing sexual needs as well, to the mutual benefit and happiness of both? Maybe this is the secret behind the success of couples who are married for decades; each was willing to put the needs of the other first, whatever those needs might be.

Next, I suggest that we court with more integrity.

Each of us has the right to expect that the person we fall in love with will indeed be the person we find ourselves living with after the marriage. There should be no unpleasant surprises. Failure to continue to be who we represented ourselves as being while we were dating might be the basic element behind much of the disillusionment that comes after marriage.

He expresses his disappointment about how when they were dating, his lady was warm and affectionate. She laughed at everything he said and enjoyed his interests and his friends. Then somewhere down the line she changed, and now he thinks he has to fight for his marital rights and put up with her pouting when he wants to go fishing with the boys.

She wonders what became of that thoughtful, considerate man she fell in love with. They cuddled and talked by the hour about everything. She loved the way he used to kiss her tenderly, hold her with no expectation beyond the pleasure of the moment, and tell her how much he looked forward to spending the rest of his life making her happy. That generous guy, who used to delight her with small gifts—a single rose with a chocolate bar tied to the stem—was replaced at some point with a miser who watched every penny.

These are exaggerated examples, of course, but I'm sure you get the point.

Too often we forget who we were back when we were dating. We were quick to please, conscious about making a good impression. We always wanted to look good for our sweethearts, and we did all we could to avoid hurting the feelings of that person who lit up our life.

Why do so many of us fail to carry those same attitudes, considerations, and behaviors into our marriage? Why are we so quick to let each other down?

A young, recently married couple stopped by our home one afternoon on their way back to college in another state. He wore jeans and a T-shirt, but he was clean-shaven and his hair was neat. She, too, wore jeans but her shirt looked as if it had lain in the dryer for days before she'd put it on. Her hair was unkempt and she didn't have on a hint of makeup. Her appearance presented a stark contrast to the lovely young woman she'd been during their courtship. She must have been aware, because as they were leaving, she said something about how awful she knew she looked but quickly added, "Oh well, nobody's going to see me."

Nobody—except the most important person in her life!

It's important, even imperative, that we keep on being the same person the other one fell in love with, retaining those qualities and attitudes we demonstrated during our courtship, and that we keep on being our best selves.

Playing old tapes—a term I learned from my counselor—can also be a significant factor affecting a new marriage. This is a phenomenon that can occur and cause real problems between couples who have been married before. It works like this: In the prior relationship, certain negative events took place and were met with predictable negative reactions. When similar situations arise in the new relationships, we play old tapes: we react in the same way as we did in the other relationship even though the circumstances, and certainly the individual involved, are completely different. Let me give you an example from the first few weeks that John and I were married.

We both had jobs where we had to report for work by eight o'clock. Our apartment was small and had only one bathroom. The first day after our weekend honeymoon, I arose, bathed, and was dressed before my new groom. By the time he was finished dressing I had breakfast on the table, and we had a cheery morning.

The second day, however, it was he who finished and started preparing breakfast first. This had me in the bathroom sobbing into a towel. The next day, it happened again, and I was so upset I got physically ill.

My sweetheart was totally confused at my distress. I was distraught, owing to my previous experiences, thinking he was probably mad at me for not being quicker about getting into the kitchen to get breakfast on the table. John also had similar experiences. Fortunately, we both learned that we were acting and responding out of old habits or prior hurts that really had nothing to do with our relationship.

If we fail to recognize when we're playing old tapes, we can complicate or even destroy the fledgling marriage we want so desperately to succeed.

There is another sensitive area, probably exclusive to widows and widowers entering into new commitments—one that could affect not only a new marriage, but also marriage prospects. It's the inclination to remember the departed spouse only in the most glowing terms. Not to seem disrespectful, but it sometimes seems that no one's spouse is perfect—until they die.

These folks might need to separate those ennobled recollections from the reality, and remember that the departed was human, just like the rest of us. If this doesn't happen, unrealistic standards for evaluating any potential marriage partner can be set up, and future relationships might be doomed before they've begun. It's unfair to both ourselves and to someone we might be able to love.

There's another caution along the same line. The tendency to glorify the dead can seemingly invalidate legitimate feelings the survivor might have in relation to lingering resentment or unresolved anger toward the one who's gone. If our mate's public image didn't match his or her persona behind the scenes, the praise and homage of others can make us feel guilty if we're still struggling with those feelings.

Unacknowledged, these feelings can eat away at the survivor, and could also affect the confidence of a potential mate, who might feel inadequate in the shadow of the one who's gone. In this case, we need to work through our own feelings and let a prospective mate know, discreetly and respectfully, about these issues.

All of us have faults. There has only been one perfect man, so it's okay to acknowledge a past mate's imperfections, even if it's only to ourselves.

Whether we're divorced or widowed, the sense of still being committed to one specific individual can linger. Dating again can feel almost like an act of unfaithfulness. We've spent most of our adult lives focusing on being devoted to one person, avoiding even the appearance of evil in our relationships with other members of the opposite sex. Now, into the mix of emotions we're already experiencing, we sometimes (erroneously) throw in feelings of disloyalty.

With our plates already full, we don't need to add unnecessarily to the burdens we're coping with. And we mustn't let others—children, family members, or friends—inflict this kind of guilt on us either. Adult children sometimes react negatively when a parent begins to show interest in someone new. "How could you even think of going out, when Dad (or Mom) has only been gone for—what is it now? Ten years?"

Younger children may suddenly seem to develop behavioral problems in response to the perceived threat of someone taking the place of the missing parent.

One divorced woman I know became very attached to a widowed friend. For several years, Jane and Mary went everywhere together, became confidants, and even took a cruise together. When Mary met and fell in love with George, Jane was devastated and even accused Mary of abandoning her.

For a time, Mary was torn between her needy friend and her new beaux, but fortunately Mary ultimately realized that she was not responsible for Jane's happiness, only for her own. She and George had eleven delightful years together before she passed away.

The decision to remarry is inherently fraught with an overwhelming number of fears and reservations. It's such a big step and carries such widespread ramifications! No one wants to make a mistake. Everyone wants to grasp at whatever happiness may come from a new union.

In the end, perhaps the solution to this quandary might be found in the scriptures: "For which of you, intending to build a tower, sitteth not down first, and counteth the cost, whether he have sufficient to finish it?" (Luke 14:28). Wise advice!

Count the cost. Consider the pros and the cons. Be as aware as possible of all the ramifications, all the ripple effects remarrying will cause. Make a decision and then take it to the Lord. Then pray and wait for an answer you can understand.

If everything seems right after that, go for it! And don't let anyone or anything dissuade you. Go forward with joy, hope, and gusto! Expect to live happily ever after, and treat each other in ways that will ensure this fairy-tale ending comes true.

Most of us must work hard to overcome our hesitancy to commit to a new relationship. Some fear being hurt again or think no other bond could possibly be as good as the first. Others fear that to love again would constitute an act of disloyalty to a departed spouse or the family we created together.

But there are many people who believe and will be quick to tell you that love can be lovelier the second time around.

Chapter 14

Children Starting Over

> When I was a child, I spake as a child, I
> understood as a child, I thought as a child.
> **I Corinthians 13:11**

When death or divorce strikes a family, children are always affected, regardless of their age. In the emotional turmoil and grief associated with both of these events, it's easy to overlook their needs. Sometimes as adults we unintentionally minimize the impact upon our younger children. Subconsciously we may think, "They're small, so their feelings are small too." Perhaps we fail to recognize that grown children are suffering. Because they are grown and have a life of their own, we think they are somewhat removed from what's happening within their first family.

We have to recognize that children experience many of the same problems as adults when coping with the death of a parent or when their mother and father divorce. Keep in mind that, just like children whose parent has died, children of divorce also live in a single-parent home, because they only live with one parent at a time.

Small children may feel abandoned by the missing parent or may feel that a parent's gone because of something the child did or didn't do. They may be afraid the remaining parent will also leave.

Adults often speak to one another in the presence or within earshot of children. These conversations involve topics that are over the heads of younger children and can be confusing or misconstrued. Children also pick up tones and inflections and recognize tension in the voices and in the body language of adults. Children of all ages, including infants, are affected by the emotional state of a parent.

There may be all kinds of unusual commotions, such as strange people coming and going from the home, but children can't always make sense of these activities. Children may be unable to form the right questions to ask, the answers to which might resolve these feelings. There are a plethora of emotions that can arise in children who are too young to verbalize their concerns.

It's important to remember that a child processes information from a child's frame of reference—his life's experiences, language limitations, and imagination. With this in mind, it's easy to understand how the snatches of information that reach a child's ears can compound the stress associated with one of these singular events.

Simply put, children need information

- in small doses
- geared to their level of understanding
- from an adult they trust
- delivered without a lot of drama

That can be a tall order for a mother or father who is barely coping from day to day or hour to hour.

Earlier we talked about getting outside intervention to help children during the transition from a two-parent family to a one-parent family. This doesn't have to be a hundred-dollar-an-hour psychiatrist. It can be a compassionate home teacher, a friendly bishop, an LDS Family Services counselor, the parents of their friends, a trusted family friend, a school teacher, a guidance counselor, or a community mental health clinician. The decisive factor in selecting someone to provide this kind of help is that he or she needs to understand the principles listed above.

The death of a parent or a divorce in the family carries with it the potential of unintentionally bringing childhood to a screeching halt. Let me give you an example from my own experience.

I grew up in what we refer to today as a dysfunctional family. (Who didn't, right?) When my mother and my only sibling, a sixteen-year-old brother, slipped away from our farm at the southern tip of New Jersey in the middle of the night, I was five years old and too young to understand their reasons. When my father discovered they were gone, a fruitless search ensued. When we returned to the house, my father built a fire, bundled me in a blanket, and sat me on a chair in front of the fireplace. He rubbed my hands and feet, and gave me a cup of warm cocoa. Then he knelt on the floor in front of me and, taking my face into his big, rough hands, he said, "Well, sweetheart, I guess you're the lady of the house now." My childhood ended on that cold October night. For the next seven years, while I lived with him, I was indeed the lady of the house. My father taught me to clean and cook, to wash clothes and iron, and even how to sew and crochet. Performing those activities was not the cause of my lost childhood, but rather it was the emotional weight of that position, as I perceived it to be.

Sometimes, because of our own devastation, we place upon children burdens that they were never intended to shoulder. This can include physical work or responsibility for siblings, both of which can restrict their own play time (play *is* work and learning to children). Some of us also burden our children with the responsibility of our emotional state as well. We say things like, "Be a good little man, now, so Mommy doesn't get one of her headaches," or "Come here and sit by Daddy so he won't feel so lonely."

We must remember which one is the grown-up, so as not to unwittingly rob our children of those precious early years that are all too quickly gone.

Another common occurrence is when the child's loyalty is split between two divorced parents. When one parent condemns the other parent in front of or directly to a child, it forces the child to take sides, perhaps to defend the disparaged parent, or even worse, to assume the role of peacemaker between two people he loves who may sound like they hate each other. No child should be placed in any of these positions, because a child is not to be used as a tool to inflict pain on another person.

If you loved someone, and other people you loved kept repeating horror stories about that individual, don't you think you might eventually start to question your ability to judge character in people? You love this person, but no one else does, so what's wrong with you? We must not undermine a child's confidence in his ability to trust his own instincts or his heart.

No matter how much we might have been hurt in a relationship, unless there are physical safety or valid mental health issues involved, children are entitled to feel equally loyal to both parents. Those who, for reasons of retaliation or spite, disregard or interfere with a child's natural right to the affection between himself and one of his parents will not only damage the child, but may themselves suffer a backlash at some time in the future, and could wind up losing the love and respect of that child.

Every child has the God-given right to his childhood, to feel and have confidence in the love of both parents, and to live in a home where peace and calm invite the presence of the spirit. Every child deserves to have experiences that will build self-esteem, to develop the skills needed as an adult, and to perceive his world as nonthreatening.

Adult children also suffer when a parent dies or there is a divorce, because we never really outgrow our need for our parents. When a parent dies, adult children progress through the stages of grief much like the surviving spouse; but they can view the situation through mature eyes and usually understand the concept of life everlasting and the eternal nature of the family. It doesn't erase the pain of the loss, but it can mitigate the suffering. Grown children can understand what is really going on because they have a bigger frame of reference than younger children and don't have to rely upon imagination or try to interpret conversations or events.

When parents divorce, adult children can be subjected to just as many conflicts as younger children. This stress may be compounded by the parents sharing of the details of the circumstances surrounding the split because they are adults.

Unfortunately, a divorce requires that one individual bring the action against the other, and even if it's a so-called no fault divorce, the parties don't usually come through it evenly in their own eyes. One person usually feels like the underdog, and when that parent deals with adult children from that position, it can affect the adult child's relationship with the other parent.

There are two sides to every story, both of which should usually be kept private. Unless there is a valid reason to convey any of the particulars, information can be doled out on a need-to-know basis. If unflattering details are known, each parent can encourage the adult children to dwell on the positive qualities of the other parent, and to incorporate into themselves the worthy characteristics, while being aware and avoiding those traits that brought about the problems.

Even though there may be no blatant vilification of the other parent, the implication still comes across loud and clear that one parent has ruined the other's life and because of this, the first parent will never be happy again. That message makes it difficult for those adult children to be glad for any good or happy things that happen to the other parent. Further, if that parent should marry again, it might also rob those children of an opportunity for a relationship with someone who might enrich their lives. It's another form of making a child take sides.

If a surviving or divorced parent begins to step out socially, adult children can sometimes respond with incredulity, as if we've lost our minds. They fail to comprehend that just because we're no longer in our twenties or thirties, we can still be lonely for companionship or feel an attraction to a member of the opposite sex.

Sometimes children of any age can interpret this renewed interest as an act of disloyalty to the parent who has died, or as a threat to the child's hope that divorced parents will reconcile and reunite the family.

Regardless of age, children are not always mature enough to understand our motivations and needs, and they may try in an assortment of ways to discourage our relationships with members of the opposite sex.

Sometimes when children are still in the home, we have to put their needs and well-being above our own, and that's as it should be. It comes with the territory, and we knew that when we decided to bring a child into the world. But if, at some point, it becomes critical that we look out for our *own* physical, emotional, and spiritual welfare, we need to remember that there can be things more damaging and more emotionally crippling than growing up in a single-parent family.

If that time ever comes, we need to remember that the other parent is also a child of God and special in the eyes of his or her children, and we need to treat and speak of that person accordingly.

The Lord has commanded children to honor their father *and* their mother—regardless of their relationship with each other (see Exodus 20:12). We may be held accountable if we do anything to interfere with their ability to keep that commandment. Even though it's terribly hard sometimes to rise above our feelings, we have an obligation to help preserve a child's connection to that other parent, regardless of that child's age.

If the other parent is not worthy of a child's love and respect, in time that love and respect might be withdrawn, but it will be because that son or daughter chooses to retreat from the relationship, not because of anything you said or did.

There are many special circumstances surrounding a child's loss of a parent, whether that separation comes because of death or divorce, and regardless of the age of the child. It may necessitate involving persons outside the immediate family, or even minimizing the appearance of our own pain for their benefit. Whatever it takes, we owe it to our children to help them get through this time with as little added stress as possible, even if it requires some sacrifice on our part, because that's what being a parent is all about.

Chapter 15
Members without Mates

> Language has created the word *loneliness* to express the pain of being alone, and the word *solitude* to express the glory of being alone.
>
> PAUL TILLICH

The sense of lost love when a spouse dies or a marriage is dissolved can leave us empty and despairing. We know that God loves us, but somehow the comfort of that knowledge can escape us when we're longing for someone to put their arms around us after a hard day. Our loneliness can seem so devastating, so profound, so complete, so utterly without relief.

These are the times when we might be the most vulnerable and when we must be the most cautious about our decisions and the paths we choose. These are the times that are fraught with the most danger, emotionally, physically, and spiritually; times when we can be most easily seduced by Satan's temptations. But these are also the times when we have the greatest opportunity to draw close to the Lord. This is one of the blessings of the promise that all things can work together for our good.

For James, a forty-five-year-old divorced man who'd never had children, loneliness was the most difficult part of becoming single. He hated being alone, and his empty house was the root of his despair.

The blessing that came out of this condition was that James turned to his Heavenly Father with a totality and a fervor he'd never anticipated possible. He said that he learned what it means to turn to God with a broken heart and a contrite spirit. How sad that it often takes a catastrophe or tragedy to bring some of us to this state.

One of my visiting teachers said that when she walked into the chapel for sacrament meeting for the first time after her divorce, she felt as if she'd been struck in the chest with a sledgehammer. She couldn't breathe, a sob caught in her throat, and she wanted to turn and run somewhere—anywhere—that would relieve the pain. Were it not for the support of compassionate friends in the ward, she'd probably still be running, she said, trying to escape that terrible sense of being alone.

For myself, I had always thought in terms of family when it came to the gospel and the Church. Everything associated with membership in the Church was a collective thing. *We* joined the Church, *we* went to the temple, *we* were sealed to our children, and *we* had family home evening. There was seldom in my mind any reminder of individuality and the Church's emphasis on the family only reinforced this inclination on my part.

A few months after my divorce, I attended the temple for the first time without my husband. It was there that I remembered that the gospel is about saving individuals. The family is referred to as the basic unit of the Church, but a role of the Church is to teach, strengthen, and encourage individuals.

The Lord wants us to form families because this association magnifies our chances for exaltation, but marriage is not a prerequisite for membership in the Church or for receiving most of the ordinances of the gospel. The Lord has promised that no blessing will be denied his worthy children, and those who don't have the chance in this life to be sealed to a mate will have that opportunity beyond the veil.

Being single in a family-oriented Church environment can be hard. Members without mates, even those who have never been married, can feel estranged in many ways from the general membership. Some Church social functions are geared to married couples, and of course, singles are invited, but many don't participate. It's difficult to have a good time when you feel like a third wheel.

Members whose mates have died are sometimes more comfortable in the Church than those who are divorced. It's easy to offer comfort to those in mourning. It's more difficult to know what to say to the person you've just discovered has been divorced. We tend to keep these things quiet until the last possible moment, so when someone appears suddenly without a wedding ring, it's only human nature for everyone to wonder, *What happened? Who initiated the proceeding? They seemed so happy! What on earth should we say?*

Sometimes other members of the Church say nothing rather than risk saying the wrong thing. To sidestep awkward situations, some may go so far as to avoid eye contact or coming into close physical contact with us. Some may even have negative feelings about us and might intentionally snub us. To others, divorce is like a virus. They fear it might be contagious.

Every member of the Church is human. Now, that may seem too obvious to warrant a formal statement, but I think it's necessary for us to remember and give the other members of the Church a little slack. I think it's the responsibility of each of us not to take offense, not to take personally behaviors that may be the result of human nature or another's insecurities or insensitivities. And we certainly must not use the discomfort of these people as an excuse to limit our own activity or participation.

Decide right away to give everyone time to get used to your situation. Things will settle down, and if you remain friendly, extending yourself to them instead of holding back and expecting that others make the first move, you will likely find that your own comfort level quickly returns.

Show compassion to these people who really want to comfort you, who would like to say or do something to let you know that they care, but who might not know how to go about it. In other words, remember the commandment to do unto others as you would have them do unto you. Once that initial discomfort and awkwardness is overcome, things will soon get back to normal.

There are wonderful social and spiritual opportunities available through the Church for previously married members. Church leaders are aware that singles have special needs. They are trying to address some of these with programs geared especially to single adults. The singles in the Church are not forgotten.

In addition to the more formalized efforts, class leaders are also encouraged to adapt lesson material to include the unique circumstances of members without mates.

There are many who have withdrawn from Church activity for one reason or other, yet stay on the periphery of the Church. Life-changing events can be the catalyst to make one of those life-defining choices to return to full activity.

Solitude, which may weigh heavily upon us now that our mate is gone, can provide the perfect opportunity to make up for lost time. We can read scriptures and other inspirational and motivational material, attend firesides and workshops, pray, and seek the Spirit, perhaps as never before.

If you've been away, returning to the safety and spiritual security of the Church could be the greatest blessing to come out of your loss. Full activity in the Church could be pivotal to your future happiness. In these times of almost unimaginable opportunities for sin and corruption, each of us needs the safety provided by living the gospel. "Return unto me, and I will return unto you, saith the Lord" (Malachi 3:7).

The Church needs you and me, and others *like* us, who have been through trials and have overcome adversity. There are people right now, and more who will be following, who need what we have to offer by virtue of our experience. There are brethren and sisters who can benefit from our example and who can be comforted, strengthened, and encouraged by us, because we have already trodden the rocky road on which they now find themselves.

Who knows? There may be someone to whom you made a promise long ago who is counting on you and what you have to give. You may hold the key to the blessing that is to come out of someone else's despair; you may be the one who can help all things work together for their good.

The membership of the Church is growing, almost faster than it can produce leadership. We are not a church whose members are all multigeneration. We are a church of converts, in the truest sense of that word. The diversity of the membership means that we need people of all backgrounds and experience to support and offer true understanding to fledgling members. We cannot hang back and expect that those good souls (who have not had the opportunity to experience all the challenges we have overcome) to be completely equipped to help those who are "coming out of the world and into the Church," bringing with them all that this phrase entails.

As members of the Church, we place a high value on marriage and family. It is ingrained in us that the family is the basic unit of the Church. Our culture abounds with the concept of a forever family, an eternal association composed of father, mother, and children. With this emphasis, it's easy for those of us who are single to lose heart and to wonder what's wrong with us.

Not everyone finds a companion with whom they can share their lives and be sealed to for time and all eternity. Some members of the Church never marry because, for whatever reason, they never found a worthy mate. Others choose to marry outside the Church, and while these members can enjoy the blessings of the temple for themselves, they may never in this earth life experience a temple marriage. Many of us have been married and divorced or widowed before having the opportunity to have the union sealed. And still others have been sealed in the temple, only to see those covenants shattered.

It's easy to overlook the fact that we chose to come to earth to obtain a physical body, knowing that we'd have to work out our salvation through a veil of forgetfulness. We knew that we would be without the benefit of sure knowledge and that we would have to rely upon our faith. We knew we'd be subjected to trials, but we believed the promise of the Father that we'd have all the tools necessary to overcome these challenges. We accepted the fact that it would be up to us to find within ourselves the right tool to handle each problem. We trusted his word that he would never give us more than we could handle with his help.

There are blessings to be found, regardless of our situation, if we have the courage and determination to find them. As single adults, we have opportunities for personal development, often unencumbered by the distractions and demands of others, that are sometimes obscured by the busyness and commotion of married life.

Remembering the divine promise that all things can work together for our good, we might eventually come to regard our single condition as a unique and special opportunity. Our timetable for our own life is not always the same as the Lord's. We've been promised that if we live for it, we will share eternity with a worthy mate, whether that person has already come and gone or whether that person is one who is waiting to be discovered somewhere in our future.

As members of the Church, we seem to be fond of declarations: the Articles of Faith, the proclamation on the family, the Relief Society declaration. With the prayer that it might help you succeed in your quest to find peace and happiness as a single adult member of the Church, the following affirmation is presented with the hope that you'll make reading it a part of every day, or that it might inspire you to compose one of your own.

Appendix A

Successfully Single—
An Affirmation of Strength

After long storms and tempests overblown,
the sun at length his joyous face doth cleare.

EDMUND SPENSER

I am a successful single adult, responsible for my own happiness. I realize that my happiness comes from within and is not dependent upon any outside influence or other person, event, or material possession.

As a successful single adult, I am responsible for *all* areas of my life, and I embrace the premise that no one else can or will make my decisions for me. I realize that I am in control of my own life and will reap the rewards or suffer the consequences of my own choices.

I realize that I must determine my own needs, foresee possible pitfalls in my life, and then provide my own support system. I am not too proud or stubborn to enlist outside help when necessary.

As a successfully single person, I do not attempt to put Band-Aids on my life experiences, covering up pain and old wounds. Instead, I deal with problems head on and don't try to avoid them. I make true healing a priority because I realize that unless these problems are resolved, they will resurface time and time again.

I am preparing for eternal life. I appreciate my singleness as an opportunity to expand my horizons and devote my efforts toward personal development, growing in the gospel, and giving service. I maintain an eternal perspective on my life, assured that all blessings will come to me based on my personal worthiness, without regard to my marital status.

As a successfully single Latter-day Saint, I seek out Heavenly Father as a full partner in all decisions, listen intently for answers and guidance, and prayerfully accept direction, even if it leads to experiences in uncharted waters. I cling to my faith in the promise that all things will work together for my good because I love the Lord. I believe that my challenges will never be more than I can successfully overcome, and by doing so, I will gain experience, strength, humility, and compassion.

I use my eternal perspective to help me rise above the adversity in my life. I practice tolerance with married members of the Church who don't quite understand my circumstances, and I support other singles by sharing my own successes and offering encouragement wherever needed, especially to newly single members, young and old, who are just beginning their own transition.

I maintain activity in the Church and participate in Church-sponsored programs and projects for single adults, knowing full well that these may at times leave something to be desired. But I go for what I might contribute, and not only for what I might take away.

I am a successful single Latter-day Saint and I realize that my future, both here on earth and in the eternities, can be virtually anything I want it to be, because I am starting over with these words of Milton written on my heart:

> *Yet I argue not*
> *Against heaven's hand or will, nor bate a jot*
> *Of heart or hope; but still bear up, and steer*
> *Right onward.*

Appendix B
My Personal Journey

This above all; to thine own self be true.

SHAKESPEARE

My Personal Goals and Self-Definition as a Single Adult

The things written in the self-definition that follows are as each line originally came out and was recorded in a section at the back of my journal. It began as a few casual observations but became a major undertaking that lasted several months.

In the beginning, it felt awkward to be writing things about myself. It was difficult to see, as time went by, that so much of what I discovered about myself was the direct result of how I had changed to accommodate others in my life.

I discovered that I seek approval; I consciously gave up personal interests, traits, and whole chunks of my personality rather than deal with the consequences that would have arisen had I not been willing to relinquish myself.

In the course of meeting others who, like myself, had been through the experience of starting over single, I found this loss of sense of self to be more common than I could have imagined, and it is for that reason that it's mentioned here.

During the course of a relationship, it's easy for some of us to lose touch with ourselves, surrendering parts of our lives that were once important to our sense of well-being, gave us immense pleasure, or brought deep satisfaction to our hearts.

This is a personal document. There is no significance in the order except that the longer I worked on it, the deeper and more clearly I saw my inner self. Each line is significant to me and has a definite relationship to my life or past experiences. Yours will be like this too. It will contain things that only you will understand—and that's as it should be.

I share it to encourage you to get in touch with who you are right now, and especially to identify the changes you want to make in yourself and in your life.

The following words are from my journal:

September 7, 1983—I have been alone now since February. It's been a difficult but amazing time during which I have experienced many emotions. I cling to my belief that I can somehow turn this experience into something good, into a time of growth and renewal, and that I can come out of this time a better, more caring, and giving person.

I cling to my faith in God and in my Savior, even though at times I think they must overestimate my strength and how much I can handle.

I am beginning to feel strongly the need to define myself and get in touch with who I really am—a single person, free of any attempts to conform myself to the demands of any other person.

A few weeks ago I began to recognize some things I've been doing just because that's what I've always done. It's set me to thinking and wondering about those qualities and characteristics that really make me, me. Now this endeavor of redefining myself—so casually begun one day over lunch—has evolved into a real project, and I am determined to find out just who I really am and what I want to be—not when I grow up, but now that I have grown up. I have to find out not only what I need to change, but I also have to discover the real me. I just hope I like what I find.

I pray for the humility to ever be able to see myself as I really am, and for the ability to discern areas where I am falling short and need to do better. I hope that this journey into myself never ends, and that I can always find more good than bad when I look inside.

May 1984—During the months that I've been working to redefine myself, I've realized that the longer I am single, the more easily I am able to see the deeper and more significant areas where I've closed off my true self.

Because of this, I've discovered that in some ways, I've become someone I don't like very much. For one thing, I've become very self-contained. I have lost the ability to express my real feelings, to the point that at times I almost choke on my disappointment or anger.

There have been times in the past when I have then transferred some of that negativity to my children, reacting negatively to situations involving them. I hate that I've done this.

Since beginning this journey of self-discovery, I've also realized that much of my current personality is actually the result of trying to deal with conflicts, or to accommodate situations in my marriage. I feel that I need to examine each of these, so I can rid myself of the last vestiges of that experience and eliminate the things that have the potential to create future problems for me or those I love.

I have a renewed realization that I am, nevertheless, important. I have legitimate needs and worth and rights as a human being, and I am an individual—not an extension of someone else. No person should ever stifle individuality to the point that he loses his personal identity, and no person has the right to require that of another.

I am profoundly impressed with the fact that despite my obvious faults and weaknesses, I still deserve to be loved, appreciated, and treated with respect, if for no other reason than because I am a child of God: unique, complex, and ever changing.

In the beginning, the things I realized about myself were—for the most part—fairly superficial. But as my confidence and self-esteem have grown, I have been able to recognize and admit things that were closer to my heart. It's been like coming out from under a cloud.

Each day I realize something new.

When I awaken each morning, I find myself smiling because I know that so much happiness is waiting for me—whatever happens! I'm even beginning to like myself again and to believe that I'm going to be okay.

No, that's not right. I'm *convinced* that I'm going to be okay!

"Me" by Me

Eternal Goal

- Return to the presence of my Heavenly Father and look into the eyes of my Savior

Life Goals

- Serve my brothers and sisters, in and out of the Church
- Strive to improve myself on a daily basis; I never want to stop growing
- Go on a mission
- Retain my temple recommend and my temple blessings—with or without a companion
- Be a temple worker when I'm too old to do much else
- Read at least four good, gospel-oriented books per year
- Read for education and recreation
- Go to Hawaii by 1985 to see daughter #3
- Make a baby afghan for each of my grandchildren
- See my children all active in the Church. (While I have no control over this, I have the faith to believe that if I do my best to live the commandments, I will be blessed for my faithfulness, as was Mosiah, to see my children truly converted. I don't want to interfere with their agency, so I pray constantly that God will send into their lives people who will be for their eternal good.)
- Continue to love and appreciate my children for the marvelous and precious individuals that they are
- Pursue my writing

Short-term Goals

- Get my credit rating in good shape
- Attend BYU Education Week in August
- Buy myself a Z car
- Type up my personal history and distribute copies to my family
- Arrange an activity for after Church each Sunday (have friends to dinner, go for a walk on the Green Belt, write letters) so I won't be lonely
- Reorganize my storage stuff
- Write six newsletters to family and friends per year
- Lose fifty pounds
- Compete in a five-mile Fun Run

Daily Goals

- Have personal prayer at least twice
- Read at least one chapter of scripture

- Maintain my personal journal
- Maintain a healthy weight
- Keep in touch with who I am and where I am going, in accordance with the choices I'm making at the present time

Optional

- Marry—if I can find a worthy mate to whom I can be equally yoked, who wants my help in becoming the best that he can be, and who is committed to helping me become the best that I can be.

Self-Definition

- These are the personality traits that make me who I am or who I'm striving to become.
- I do *not* like Roquefort dressing! (Twenty-six years without Ranch—wasted!)
- I am very neat and well organized; I don't function well in chaos.
- I like to get up early and go to bed early. I wake up happy!
- I like to read and then talk about it with someone who cares about what I think.
- I love small children and old people.
- I hate to be put down.
- I want to sing in a choir.
- I like kittens and cats and dogs—if they're housebroken.
- I need eight to nine hours of sleep to function at my best.
- Once I make up my mind about something, I like to get on with it.
- I love good art—especially the old masters (but not abstract)—romantic poetry, and classical music.
- I love to dance, and I am good at it.
- I like people and *must* be involved with others.
- I have little tolerance for stupid people who remain stupid by choice.
- I am terrified of worms, snakes, and being physically restrained.
- I am outspoken but try not to be obnoxious about it.
- I will answer honestly when asked a question, even if it's personal.
- I do not play my cards close to my chest. I am very open about everything. (Maybe too open?)
- I love to give gifts and to do things for people. I tend to overdo sometimes.

- I have very few things that I would not give away to someone who I felt needed it more than I.
- I am a goal setter!
- My happiness is not connected with things, and I do not need money to be happy.
- I don't like debt that threatens my security.
- I like to travel, play games, read, talk about deep subjects, and ride motorcycles.
- I love walking on the beach or in the woods.
- I am very affectionate and need to be touched and cuddled.
- I love to talk and talk, getting into myself and those I care about.

Qualities I Desire in a Future Marriage Partner

- He must love the Lord more than he loves me.
- He must be active, converted, and committed to the gospel.
- He must want a celestial, eternal relationship and be willing to work toward that.
- He must be affectionate, kind, patient, tolerant (not a nit-picker), and peace-loving.
- He must not exercise unrighteous use of his priesthood authority.
- He must be compassionate, love people, and be willing to help and serve other children of God. He must be a good father— loving and accepting of his children regardless of their choices.
- He must be intelligent, neat, and clean. He must care about his appearance.
- He must be able to make decisions.
- He must live within his income. (His income bracket doesn't matter.)
- He must be considerate; I will not do all the giving again.
- He must be willing to have me involved in his life, and he must not use me as a convenience.
- He must have a sense of humor; life is too difficult to not laugh at it.
- He must encourage me in my personal development.
- He needs to assume the leadership role in the family.
- He must want and appreciate a clean, well-organized home, and contribute to that effort.

- He must love music.
- It would be really nice if he loved to sing or played the piano or the guitar.

I would like a man who is warm, affectionate, and passionate and who is not passive. One who appreciates that sex is a powerful bond in a marriage. *I must feel loved—not just my body.*

I would like a man who needs to continue to grow toward God-hood, and who would help me do the same.

I would like a man who loves truth and goodness, beauty, and peaceful things. A man who will accept all the love and devotion I have to give and who will respect me as a daughter of God, appreciating me for the good qualities that I have, and who will help me overcome my weaknesses.

I would like a man who won't fold up in a crisis and leave the survival to me, but who also has the humility to turn to the Lord in tough times; a man who is willing to admit mistakes and forgive both himself and others and go forward; a man who is not too proud to cry when he's hurt or touched by the Spirit; a man who loves and appreciates himself as a son of heavenly parentage and who understands his eternal potential.

I need a companion who will lead me back into the presence of God and who wants the journey to be filled with joy.

Postscript

On July 18, 1985, I was blessed to marry the man described above. I'm so thankful that I was able to recognize him when he came along, but only because I'd already written about him, without realizing it at the time. It could have been so different. On May 4, 1996, my beloved and I were sealed for time and all eternity the Boise Idaho Temple. Thank you, Heavenly Father!

About the Author

Teena Read was born in New Jersey and migrated through New York, Vermont, Florida, California, and Oregon on her way to Idaho, where she settled in 1976. She and her husband, John H. Read married in 1985. Between them, they have seven children, fourteen grandchildren, and three great-grandchildren. Since leaving her "real" job, Teena divides her time between CEO Inc., a business management consulting firm she and John began in 1999, and pursuing her writing. She is also the author of *The Mormon Way* and *Family Emergency Preparedness Plan*. You can contact her at ceoinc@cableone.net.

0 26575 51289 2